Unde ... *Dog's Behaviour*

Understanding your Dog's Behaviour

by

Alice Heim

Open Books

First published in 1984 by
Open Books Publishing Limited
West Compton House, nr. Shepton Mallet, Somerset

Typeset by V & M Graphics Ltd, Aylesbury, Bucks
Printed by A. Wheaton & Co. Ltd, Exeter

To Eleanor and Martin,
Felicity and John

Contents

ACKNOWLEDGEMENTS

This book has entailed far more research than I had originally envisaged. It has prompted me to get in touch with policemen, sheep dog handlers and shepherds, guide dog trainers, and those engaged in the 'hearing dogs for the deaf' movement. The people whom I consulted gave generously of their time and they instructed me clearly and enthusiastically. When, later, I sought comments on the chapters I had written, they promptly produced constructive criticism.

My grateful thanks, therefore, go to Commander Cree and Inspector Nicolson of the Metropolitan Police, who put me in touch with Chief Inspector A. E. Clarke, Chief Instructor at the main Police Dog Training Establishment. He and his various colleagues were welcoming, instructive and kind.

My helpful contacts regarding sheep dogs were Mr Norman Seamark, sheep farmer and trainer of several sheep dog champions, and Mr John Clark of the Agricultural Research Council's Institute of Animal Physiology. Both were highly co-operative and informative.

I also visited one of the Training Centres of the Guide Dogs for the Blind Association. Once again, I was made most welcome – this time by Mr Stephen Wright, Controller of the Leamington Training Centre. He proved an admirable guide to the intricacies of selecting and training guide dogs and matching them to their future owners.

My fourth visit was to Mr Tony Blunt who – with his Placement Counsellor, Miss Gillian Lacey – explained to me the aims of hearing-dogs for the deaf and demonstrated the skills of several of their canine trainees. I gratefully acknowledge the expertise of all these people, their capacity for getting the principles across to a novice and their useful criticism of the first drafts of my chapters on working dogs.

I wish to express thanks, too, to Dr Bruce Fogle, veterinary surgeon and writer, for his help and for his introduction to Ms Dorothy Walster of the Scottish Health Education Unit, Edinburgh, who provided me with interesting literature on the dog as therapist. Warmest thanks go also to Mrs Eleanor Burgess for reading the typescript and spotting a number of errors and ambiguities; and to Mrs Margaret Elvin for her help with correcting the proofs. Finally, especial gratitude to my friend Dr Caroline Manser, BVSE, Ph.D., MRCVS, for reading the first scruffy draft of the book and for her immensely valuable comments and additions. Appropriately enough, she and I were introduced to each other by our respective dogs – long ago, when walking them on the fen!

A.W.H.
April, 1983

Illustrations
The publishers are most grateful to the following for the use of illustrations:
Commissioner of Police of the Metropolis (9-11 and 14); Guide Dogs for the Blind Association (19-24); Hearing Dogs for the Deaf Association (25 and 26); Marc Henrie (1-5, 8, 12, 13, 15, 16 and 18); Norman Seamark (17); Vidocq Picture Library (6 and 7).

CHAPTER 1

Introductory

In this book I am endeavouring to see things *from the dog's point of view*: hence the title, *Understanding your Dog's Behaviour*. The better you understand your dog, the better he will understand you. The relationship is reciprocal – as indeed is any relationship between two living beings. But it is possible and perhaps enlightening to consider one aspect at a time.

We understand other people (insofar as we *do* understand them) by interpreting their behaviour, that is, their movements, their facial expression, their activities – and, of course, their speech. Some of us interpret these things better than others, just as some are better than others at driving a car, hanging a picture or learning a new language. Our skills are largely dependent on our interests and these differ markedly from person to person. Indeed, it is odd that the word 'interesting' should be so widely accepted and used since it is equally widely accepted that one man's meat (ie. taste or interest) is another man's poison (ie. dislike or boredom).

Our understanding of domesticated dogs is also dependent on our interpreting their behaviour: this is even truer of dogs than of people, as dogs do not talk. At least they do not use speech as humans do – although, as we shall see, dogs do understand human language to a remarkable degree, when given the opportunity: and they can also express themselves very clearly, if we take the trouble to observe and respond to their behaviour. One often hears it said of a dog, 'He can almost speak' or 'She can do everything but talk'. What the speaker means by this is that the dog *tells* us by his movements, his facial expression and his activities what he means if we will only learn to listen and look. Learning to listen and look, that is, to interpret the dog's behaviour, is what it is all about.

I say 'by *his* movements' etc. rather than 'by his/her movements' because if I insert the alternative word each time, the writing becomes jerky and cumbersome. Thus the masculine terms are used throughout to include dogs and bitches, in the same way as the word 'mankind' is generally used to include men and women.

To return to the dog's movements, expression and activities: let us consider some examples of these. Movements include tail-wagging, pricking up ears, scratching, panting, body-shaking, nose-twitching. Facial expression is harder to designate because it is less objective. There would be little controversy about whether a dog is wagging his tail or pricking his ears, etc., but as soon as it is a matter of determining whether he is looking alert, disappointed, curious, sympathetic, welcoming or in pain, doubt may be voiced – particularly by non-dog-lovers, experimental psychologists and professional sceptics.

I would agree that it is not always easy to interpret the facial expression of a dog (or, for that matter, of a human being) in isolation. If all one could see were the isolated head, the rest of the body being hidden and the whole context unknown, it might well be difficult to infer what the individual is feeling. But in practice a dog's total behaviour-pattern is observable – his movements, his facial expression and his activities – and these various cues generally confirm one another. Indeed it is not possible to draw a clearcut line between them: ear-pricking and nose-twitching (described above as movements) contribute to facial expression; body-shaking and tail-wagging (also described as movements) could arguably be classed as activities. What then do I have in mind when I talk of activities? – I mean, for instance, walking or running, eating and drinking, mating, scratching at the door, leaping into a car, fighting.

In this chapter I confine myself to instinctive or unlearned behaviour. Activities that are taught, will be considered in a later chapter. But I must again stress that such divisions are arbitrary. The purist may well complain that leaping into a car is scarcely an 'instinctive' activity – since the instincts of a species go back centuries, if not longer, whereas the car is a comparatively recent invention. I use this example, however, because many a dog will jump into the car if he suspects that his owners are about to drive away without him. Far from having taught the dog to do this, his owner may find such behaviour highly embarrassing! Similar considerations apply to snuffling or scratching at the door. Other activities, such as urinating and defecating – whilst undoubtedly instinctive, in the sense that they are unlearnt and common to all animals – get modified in the domesticated dog, in that he learns (with impressive adaptability) when and where to perform these actions. He is obviously not taught *how* to relieve himself but he is taught that it is forbidden indoors and, even, that it is forbidden in certain places out-of-doors.

It may seem strange that in my examples of doggy behaviour as illustrations of how *he* teaches *us* two-way communication, I have made no mention of barking, growling or whining, and other sounds voluntarily produced by dogs. In view of the fact that communication between humans is largely (though not exclusively) verbal, it may well appear doubly strange. I have so far omitted canine vocalisation on two grounds. First, I do not wish to give the impression that it can be equated with human speech. Domesticated dogs do acquire a 'human vocabulary' but it is a 'recognition' vocabulary, analogous to that of a 12-18 month child. Secondly, whilst it is no overstatement in my view to claim that dogs can communicate with people, they do so primarily in the ways suggested above, namely by their (usually silent) behaviour. But sometimes, as will be seen later, dogs do communicate audibly with people. In the next chapters we shall look more closely at movements, facial expression and activities, and see what we can learn from them.

CHAPTER 2

Types of Normal Behaviour: Movement

My list of tail-wagging, ear-pricking, nose-twitching, scratching, panting and body-shaking is far from exhaustive. Dogs indulge in many other voluntary movements but these six are not chosen at random: they are selected as being typical means of communication between the dog and his owner, and other human friends.

Tail-wagging takes pride of place because this movement as an expression of pleasure is essentially dog-like. As Lewis Carroll's Cheshire Cat pointed out to Alice long ago, 'a dog's not mad' and 'a dog growls when it's angry and wags its tail when it's pleased. Now' said the Cat, '*I* growl when I'm pleased, and wag my tail when I'm angry...' '*I* call it purring, not growling', said Alice. 'Call it what you like', said the Cat.

It is commonly believed that dogs wag their tails when they are pleased and this belief is wholly justified, but the matter is more complex than that. Dogs have at least four different kinds of tail-wag and each signifies a different state of mind. They may be termed, respectively, joyful, pleading, questioning and reassuring.

The tail-wag of joy is usually involuntary and unselfconscious. (Those who claim that self-consciousness is an exclusively human trait lack perceptiveness and empathy with their dog.) It may be seen when the dog is told that a walk is imminent; or when a well-loved friend comes to the house; or when a stick is thrown, at the dog's request (wag) and he manages to catch it (wag-wag). The mere announcement of 'dinner' will produce a tail-wag, long before the food is actually presented. Even when considering the expression of joy, to restrict oneself to the term 'tail-wagging' is to over-simplify. Some dogs, such as Pugs and Boxers – whose tail has been abbreviated by nature or man – eloquently agitate their hindquarters; others wave their tail round in a circular motion and others thump the ground with their tail. The last, of course, is possible only when seated or lying down, and this more restful procedure is likely to be adopted only when he is growing old. Tail-wagging is not the *only* means of expressing pleasure: in a young dog it is often accompanied by ecstatic leaps and, at all ages, a brightening of the eye and some tensing of the body may be seen. The following account of differing tailwags is applicable to those dogs whose tails are at least a few inches long.

The *pleading* tailwag differs from the joyful in style and in situation. It is usually initiated by the dog himself – as opposed to being stimulated by some change of circumstances. It is a smaller, more deliberate and controlled movement; and it may denote, for instance, 'couldn't we have a game now?' or 'isn't it dinner time?' or 'surely it's high time for our guests to leave?' or even 'I'm very sorry – please forgive me!' if the dog thinks, correctly or incorrectly, that he has offended you. This wag is more selfconscious than the wag of joy: the dog appears to be aware of the movement and to switch it on and off in a purposeful manner.

He will occasionally use a similar technique when

1. *Tailwagging with pleading expression.*

uncertain of the intentions of another dog. The same small, somewhat jerky, slightly downward tailwag will appear, sometimes accompanied by a placatory little whine. Interestingly enough, the other dog does not always understand. Perhaps the best adjective here is to call it an *appeasing* tailwag – and it contains an element of hope rather than joy.

The pleading or appeasing tailwag closely resembles the *questioning* tailwag, both in movement and in situation. Typical examples of such questioning are (the dog indicating) 'wherever did that ball go? – I *must* find it' or '*what* does she want me to do – I'd like to help' or 'is that the garden gate being opened? – and is that Aunt Mabel arriving?'. Putting it into words in this way looks extremely anthropomorphic, that is, it looks as though I am attributing to the dog ideas, feelings and anticipations that are often thought to be the prerogative of human beings. That is, of course, precisely the case: I am doing so because I believe that this is the only way to explain all aspects of a dog's behaviour.

I do not claim that dogs possess as great a capacity for *abstract thought* as does the average human being or that all dogs show loving understanding to the same extent – any more than all persons do.

My justification for this anthropomorphism (to which we shall return later) is threefold. In the first place, if we are discussing ways of understanding our dog, these must necessarily be expressed in words. Secondly, subsequent events often confirm our initial interpretation: that sound you failed to hear *was* caused by the opening of the garden gate and it is, indeed, Aunt Mabel who is visiting you. Thirdly, as I said above, ideas and anticipations *are often thought* to be the prerogative of human beings.

I believe that we are mistaken in thinking that we have, uniquely, the capacity for entertaining such concepts. Dogs (and some other animals) who are talked to, and responded to, develop quite a large recognition-vocabulary and means of conveying their own feelings and reactions. As with children, if they are *not* spoken to and responded to, they will fail to fulfil their potential; and, again as in children, immense differences among individuals are found.

The tailwag of *reassurance* is even more deliberate. Some dogs will seek to console you in this way when you accidentally tread on their paw. 'It's all right', indicates the dog, positively apologising for his involuntary yelp. 'You didn't mean to do it and it doesn't really hurt!' (Some dogs, on the other hand, respond to such an incident with a growl and a snap – the equivalent of 'Careful! You'd better not do that again!') This tailwag will also be used when he feels that his companion is worried or depressed. He will approach her (the feminine pronoun is used here to clarify the sense), perhaps placing a paw on her knee or arm if accessible, and wag his tail gently and meaningfully, fully aware of what he is doing. It is not wholly fanciful to picture his message along the lines of, 'Cheer up ... it's not so bad ... I'm with you, as ever ...' Once again this is undeniably anthropomorphic. I would not claim that even the most intelligent and well-educated dog would go far in philosophy or science or art, but I have no doubt that their reasoning and their feelings differ from ours in degree rather than in kind.

Let us now consider ear-pricking and nose-twitching jointly, for they often occur simultaneously and they are usually brought into play when the dog becomes aware of something interesting or unexpected or suspicious in the offing. Even those who pooh-pooh the notion of a dog's sharing to any degree a human's capacity for feeling and for thinking – even they admit the immense superiority of the dog's sense of hearing and of smell, over our own. The extent of this superiority is unimaginable for most of us: it implies whole worlds which we cannot begin to appreciate.

Their hearing excels ours in both acuity and range. They are able to hear tiny noises of which we are quite unaware, even if actually listening for them; and they can hear sounds of such high frequency that they are way beyond the range of human ability – even the ability of a child (for our sense of hearing is more acute and higher ranging in childhood than when we are older). The 'dog-whistles' used by some shepherds and some dog-trainers emit an extremely high-pitched sound, that dogs (and some other animals) hear and respond to although they, again, lose some of this capacity with advancing years. The sensitivity of the dog's ear is not only a matter of detecting very soft or very high sounds. Dogs also have an extraordinary ability (extraordinary by human standards) of discriminating among noises that may sound identical to us. There are well-authenticated cases of dogs in war-time differentiating, for instance, between the sound of enemy aircraft and the aircraft of their own country, and of discriminating between the sound of one motor-bicycle (that of the dog's master) and another motor bicycle of the same make. Many breeds of dog can twitch their ears forwards and backwards, upwards and sideways, when they hear, or suspect that they are hearing, intriguing sounds. This is the briefest way of describing what happens when a dog suddenly rises, pricks up his ears, puts his head first on one side and then on the other –

2. *On the alert – ears pricked, head turned.*

evidently to focus better the source and the identity of the sound, which his human companion may or may not hear – and then perhaps makes for the door, wagging his tail, clearly indicating that someone has come home, and he thinks he knows who it is. He is usually right.

Nose-twitching is a similar phenomenon. But while we can conceive of the possession of more acute hearing than that of human ears – dogs' hearing differing from ours in degree – we cannot begin to imagine the sensitivity of their sense of smell. It is so greatly superior to ours that it is, in effect, almost a different sense. A dog's sense of smell differs *qualitatively* from ours. It yields him information and pleasures and horrors of which we can have no inkling.

Hence his habit of twitching his nostrils. Nose-twitching is to smelling as ear-pricking is to hearing. And the combination of these two great dog-senses accounts for a lot of your dog's behaviour. When something interests us, we think it over and we talk it over: when something interests a dog, he smells it over and listens to it, with single-minded intentness. He may well also *look* at it (and touch it tentatively with his paw). Some breeds of dog, such as whippets and sheep-dogs in youth and middle-age, have vision superior to that of humans, and others do not – the latter relying on their two remarkable canine gifts, which again vary from breed to breed and from individual to individual. Dogs, however, will share their interest with you, by means of their behaviour, if you are prepared to observe and interpret their movements. He is always prepared to share *your* interests – although he may find some of them rather odd – provided you give him the opportunity.

It is sometimes claimed that dogs have tele-pathic abilities or 'second sight'. This may be true of a few individual dogs just as it seems to be true of a small minority of people. But in my view many cases of apparent extra-sensory perception in dogs can be explained in terms of their fine sense-organs and the constant use dogs make of them.

Dogs scratch themselves when some part of their body itches or tickles. This may be due to fleas – and even the most aristocratic and well-groomed dog is liable to pick up an occasional flea – or to some skin infection, such as eczema, or to the sensation of water drying on the body, after a dog has been swimming or out in the rain. He may, in such cases, rub himself against walls or furniture rather than use a paw to scratch himself: he is, in effect, asking you to dry him. A brisk rub-down with a rough towel should effectively end his rubbing against things.

It may appear strange to group scratching with tail-wagging and ear-pricking, but it is relevant for it too is a response to a stimulus and – if a satisfactory relationship has been established – the dog will be communicating something to you, as well as gaining some physical relief, by scratching or rubbing himself. He is probably asking you to remove the flea, to groom him or to dry him.

It is true that a dog who does not have a close relationship with his owner will also scratch himself, when he itches. But he will not gaze meaningfully at her (the owner) during the scratching, for she has not taught him that she can and will relieve the itch. Some dog-owners say comfortably, 'Oh, he loves a good scratch', but I think they are deluding themselves. The dog's 'enjoyment' of scratching is no greater than our

3. *Scratching ear with hind leg.*

4. *Panting.*

enjoyment of scratching a mosquito-bite, i.e. it brings a temporary relief followed by a still stronger itch – or worse.

If the dog scratches himself for more than a few seconds, and if he continually repeats the procedure, he probably needs your help. If he concentrates on scratching an ear, he may have contracted an ear-infection, in which event he will probably require the expertise of a vet. The dog is usually quick to let you know if he has ear trouble for he not only scratches but he also shakes his head, and holds it one side and – if his breed allows him to control the position of his ears – he may 'wear' one up and the other down.

Panting, again, is different in intent from the other types of behaviour and – like tail-wagging – it is sometimes under voluntary control and sometimes not. A dog will of course pant involuntarily if he has been running fast, or jumping, and he is out of breath. He will pant involuntarily also in very hot weather, as this is his sole means of reducing his body-heat (apart from finding cold water or shade). When we become over-hot, we lose heat by sweating; many areas of our skin become damp or even wet. But dogs do not sweat through their fur-coats, although they do to some extent through their paws. Their main means of reducing heat is through their tongues and this is why dogs tend to pant, open-mouthed, in hot weather. This is as involuntary as is their panting when breathless.

There is, however, a third kind of panting which is, to some extent, within their control. Thus dogs will sometimes affect a kind of simulated panting, as an expression of eagerness or intense interest. If one says to him, 'We'll go for a walk soon' or 'Aunt Mabel is coming to tea', he will very likely begin to pant briefly, and his eyes will brighten; and when the expected ring at the door is heard, he will pant eagerly as he hurls himself towards the front door. It is roughly the equivalent of a child who jumps up and down shouting 'goody!'

Last on my list is body-shaking. As is well-known, dogs do this on emerging from water – usually in close proximity to their owner or indeed to any fully-clothed, dry person who may be available! It is a kind of reflex action in response to being partially or wholly wet. But dogs will also shake themselves in similar fashion, after any event which has necessitated immobility or concentration. Thus they may shake themselves immediately after having had a pill administered or after their ears have been treated or just after they have been groomed. If interpretation is permissible here, this sort of body-shaking seems to express 'Fine, that's over, now I can relax'.

I have described six types of simple behaviour, all of which may be observed in the normal, healthy dog. But most of them do not occur in isolation, as my account would perhaps seem to suggest. For instance, tail-wagging, ear-pricking and nose-twitching may well be displayed simultaneously in certain situations. When wishing to interpret what a dog (or any other animal) is feeling, we have to consider the total picture – not isolated aspects of behaviour – and the context, the latter including his age, breed and previous experience as well as the present circumstances.

Two types of more complex behaviour that are normal and often exhibited are, respectively, *territorial* and *guarding*. A great many species (including mankind) feel strongly about their own particular bit of territory, and the dog is no

5. *Dog shaking water from its coat.*

exception. According to his breed and his living accommodation, he may behave territorially about his room, flat, car, house-and-garden – or even his whole street (unwarrantedly) or his farm or small-holding (justifiably). Warranted or not, it is a strong propensity and one that usually develops with maturity, or younger, manifesting itself without any special training. It accounts for the fact that most dogs will give warning when anybody is entering, or even approaching, their dwelling – whether legally or illegally. It accounts too for the occasional vigorous attack that one dog will launch on another, if a new dog takes up its abode in the other's home, or if he is visited by a guest-plus-dog. Territorial behaviour of this kind is almost always sparked off by invasion by a dog of the same sex. Dogs will rarely assault a dog of opposite sex, either at home or out-of-doors.

The defence of home-ground may consist of barking, growling, hackles-raising and, on occasion, physical attack on a person. This does not happen when the person – or the incoming dog – is a familiar friend. It is clearly a complex behaviour-pattern and, equally clearly, it is an instinctive reaction – and it can of course be strengthened if the owner is specially keen to do so.

Dogs should not be punished for manifesting territorial behaviour for they instinctively feel it to be part of their raison d'être, and it may indeed prove useful to their owner. However, a dog may need to be restrained if he is too aggressive in his defence of home. He has to learn the difference between welcome guest or regular tradesman, on the one hand, and thief-in-the-night, on the other.

A second type of complex behaviour is *guarding*. This is related but not identical to territorial

6. *Dog at ease but watchful.*

7. *Dog aroused and ready to move.*

behaviour. Guarding is concerned rather with people – notably the owner and his immediate family – and with objects belonging to them. Thus it may occur far from home. I remember once observing at a railway station a young woman travelling with two small children, two suit-cases and a dog. Miraculously a helpful porter appeared, and, to the woman's obvious relief, he took the suit-cases from her. The dog, however, became wildly excited: he tugged at the lead, barking furiously and tried to attack the porter – *guarding* the cases which had been removed from his owner. Sometimes dogs adopt such forceful guarding behaviour towards their owner or their owner's child, that spouse or friend can scarcely get a look-in!

CHAPTER 3

Types of Normal Behaviour: Facial Expression and Vocalisation

We will now consider the dog's facial expression and vocalisation. In some ways these do resemble people's modes of expressing themselves but obviously not in all. Barking is pretty rare in human beings! - although the whining of a puppy is sometimes reminiscent of a baby's crying.

Dogs who spend a lot of time with responsive people naturally pick up and imitate more human cues than do those who live mainly alone (an unsuitable life for a sociable creature) or those who spend their time with other dogs. Several friends have remarked that my dog, Marcus, has 'a very expressive face'. One or two have even commented that 'it's so funny to see a human expression on a dog's face!' I think the reason for this expressiveness is twofold: first, Marcus is my constant companion and, as such, I talk to him much of the time and frequently exchange glances with him. Secondly, he is a Border Collie and members of this breed are particularly responsive, adaptable and eager to please. He, too, will exchange glances and will earnestly watch people's faces to learn what they are feeling - and, sometimes, to indicate what *he* wishes to communicate.

In almost all dogs, however, a brightening of the eyes is observable when they are pleased about something. They almost smile: indeed some dogs of my acquaintance actually raise their upper lip in welcome, while the whole of their other end is gyrating with delight, as they greet a welcome guest.

The brightening of the eye happens, of course, in humans too. A further similarity is the occasional raising of a dog's eyebrows, when he is surprised or incredulous. Marcus does this to me when I say absentmindedly, 'Now we'll go upstairs' – when we *are* actually upstairs at that moment. It is only when I see his questioning look that I realise what it is that I have said. This sort of experience is not limited to one place or one person: it is simply an illustration of a dog's attentiveness and visible reaction. When I hastily correct my statement to 'I mean *downstairs*', Marcus relaxes, his eyebrows drop back to their usual position and he begins trotting down the stairs.

Just as a dog will raise his eyebrows when surprised, so will he raise his voice when indignant. If a dog barks once or twice at the garden door asking to be let in, his third or fourth bark will probably be higher in pitch, showing his indignation at being made to wait. Again, just as a child's lips will part sometimes in moments of pleasurable excitement, so will a dog's mouth slightly open at such times, and he may pant briefly – or affect a sniff or a mini-sneeze – to share his pleasure with you or merely signify his assent. Coupled with these facial expressions are found the raising of the head, the pricking of ears and the body-tensing, already mentioned.

The signs of depression or disappointment are complementary to those of joy. The eyes appear duller, the head and tail droop – indeed the whole body seems to sag and lose its elasticity. If he moves, he does so slowly; but he will very likely lie down and stay down – head and tail as immoveable as his body. This attitude is very different from that of the dog who is lying down in response to an order. In that event, his head is up and his eyes are bright and alert, eagerly awaiting the command or the permission to rise.

As I said earlier, barking should not be equated with human speech. Certain breeds of dog, notably the Basenji and the Australian Dingo, never bark but this does not imply that they lack intelligence or the ability to communicate with people.

Perhaps different barks signify different messages but, if so, even dogs sometimes misunderstand the import. Some dogs left in a car will bark at every dog that passes. To judge from the total behaviour of the dog-in-car – and this is the only permissible way to make a judgement – this sometimes denotes, 'You're on my territory: get out!', sometimes, 'Hallo – nice to see you!', and sometimes it merely signifies a welcome relief from boredom. Barking sometimes indicates a warning, and it sometimes denotes playfulness on the part of the barker.

If a dog rushes towards another dog (or a person), head down, hackles raised, tail held stiffly, combining barks with growls – this probably does mean that he wants to attack, but barking alone certainly does not necessarily indicate aggression, though people unused to dogs often infer this; and their apprehension may stimulate aggression on the part of the dog. Barking does not have one and only one significance. It is sometimes welcoming, sometimes curious and sometimes it is simply a symptom of general excitement.

8. Dog snarling and showing teeth – body and legs braced.

Growling, on the other hand, does usually denote a threat or at least a warning. Puppies will emit mock growls in play – their play being a kind of preparation for adult life. But the total picture is different, for the playing puppy will probably be relaxed, tailwagging and tumbling about with the touching unco-ordination of the very young. Whereas the adult dog who means business will growl, raise his hackles, stiffen his legs and body, and very likely, show his teeth in a snarl. It is a warning to be respected, if he is threatening you. If, on the other hand, he is threatening another dog, it is best not to interfere, if they are of roughly equal size and fully-grown, are in open country and on neutral ground, and are both off the lead. Actual fighting is more likely if either or both dogs are on the lead or if either dog is on the other's territory, or if you hurriedly intervene.

Given plenty of space and no human interference they may content themselves with stiff-legged growling – and finally part, both feeling that honour is satisfied. It is as true in the canine world as in the human world that face-saving is of major importance and that it takes two to make a quarrel. Some dogs do actively enjoy a fight, however unprovoked. Some, however, without necessarily being cowardly, take no pleasure in fighting. Such dogs will often stand stock-still, very likely turning their head away from the would-be aggressor – or they may roll over on their back in placating submission, thus usually avoiding confrontation. But if they turn tail and run away, the threatener will be greatly tempted to pursue and attack.

Puppies are easily frightened and, in menacing circumstances, a young puppy should be picked up and protected by his owner – just as the puppy would be in very early days by his mother. It is well-known that the female of the species will attack with great spirit if she suspects, rightly or wrongly, that her young are threatened.

Most householders believe – with reason – that owning a dog is a deterrent to burglars. This is true not only of big dogs with a reputation for fierceness such as Dobermanns and Alsatians (otherwise known as German Shepherds). It is true also of little dogs and gentle dogs *because of their bark* (or, in the case of very small dogs, their yapping). The majority of housedogs will give tongue when someone unexpectedly enters the house; many will bark whenever there is a knock or ring at the door. They should not be discouraged from doing this for it may prove useful, and the dog sees it as part of his job. Dogs have been known too to wake the household – and to save lives – by barking, or howling, at the onset of fire or gas-leakage. If your dog, in puppyhood, does not seem to like the sound of his own voice, and he looks abashed on the rare occasions when he gives tongue, it is a good idea to reward him – with a pat or a biscuit or a dog-choc – so that he learns that an occasional bark is acceptable. These innately quiet dogs will gradually learn in which situations barking is desirable, and there is no risk of their taking to vocalising over-time!

More difficult is the case of the naturally noisy dog: he who barks at everything and, apparently, at nothing. Such dogs will bark – not merely when someone walks up the garden path, but when anyone has the temerity to walk past the house or to have a conversation in the street. On a picnic, he barks if anybody comes within 20 yards of 'his family'. He will bark at the slightest sound. He is

easily excited by small happenings and his immediate reaction, when excited, is to give tongue.

It is quite clear what *not* to do, if you have a dog
of this persuasion: do *not* attempt to distract him by
means, say, of offering a dog-biscuit or throwing a
ball. He enjoys such overtures and he therefore
takes them as *rewards* for his barking and he will be
likely to bark more frequently and loudly than
ever, if he gets rewarded for it.

If your dog is too fond of the sound of his own
voice, say *no*! whenever he barks without good
reason; administer a smack on the side of his
bottom; banish him temporarily from the room, if
the noise is taking place at home. If it occurs during
a picnic or during a walk on the common,
immediately put him on the lead for a short time.
Your dog has to learn that barking is acceptable in
some situations but not in others. He can be taught
this but the lesson may need time and patience.

Under vocalisation, neither howling nor whining
have been discussed since these are not normal in
the adult, healthy dog. Whining is common in
puppies when they first leave their home and their
mothers – especially at night. This is readily
understandable: they feel strange and lonely and
they are pleading for the habitual scents and sounds
that are lacking – and also for company. At bedtime,
after having taken the young dog into the garden or
round the block, leave him in a room which has
become familiar to him during the day – but which
does not contain precious or fragile objects! Provide
him with a warm, dry, draught-free bed of some
kind and spread several thicknesses of newspaper on
the floor – for puppies cannot be continent
throughout the night, during their first few
months.

If the young dog whines or howls during the first night or two, do not succumb to the temptation to take him into your bedroom, unless you are prepared to let him sleep with you for the rest of his life. Puppies and dogs do not understand the concept of 'just this once' or 'only for a week', any more than human babies do. On the matter of sleeping accommodation, begin as you mean to go on.

The young dog may also whine or howl when you go out and leave him on his own during the day: he has to learn to accept being alone for certain periods. These should not be too long, however (not more than an hour or two) and he should not be castigated for behaving like the baby he is.

Once he has settled down; once he begins to mature and to know what goes on in his new home, howling should be a thing of the past and whining should occur very rarely. He might give a little whine when he needs to go out to relieve himself – whilst an older dog might scratch at the door – or he might remind you that it is dinner-time by giving vent to a brief, begging whine but, if all is well, he should grow out of this in due course. Howling or whining in the adult dog are pathological, and suggest that something is wrong with the way he is treated or that the dog is himself unwell. Communication between dog and human being is a reality and is, ideally, a two-way process but, on the dog's side, it consists more of his gait and movements than of his vocalisation.

CHAPTER 4

Types of Abnormal Behaviour

In the last two chapters I described types of normal behaviour, that is, typical movements displayed and sounds made by dogs when in good mental and physical health. But a dog is not always in the peak of condition – and some dogs spend much of their time being miserable or scared or ill. This may be because they have been neglected or ill-treated, or it may be that they have an innate tendency towards gloom or timidity or disease. Such dogs exhibit various types of pathological (abnormal) behaviour and, in this chapter, I discuss some of these ways of behaving.

It is important to recognise these symptoms because, if they occur in your own dog, you will wish to discover the cause – if there is one – and cure it. If, on the other hand, these signs occur in the case of a puppy in a litter, one of whose members you are thinking of acquiring, you would probably do better to select one of the other puppies.

I well recall a friend of mine who was devoted to dogs and, having decided to purchase a Cocker Spaniel, she went along to kennels of good repute to choose him. She had already decided to have a dog rather than a bitch. The puppies were about six weeks old. Most of them were animatedly playing with one another: chasing, tumbling over them-

selves and their siblings, enjoying mock battles –
and these trotted up to the stranger and the
breeder, wagging their tiny tails, expressing curio-
sity and welcome. One, however, backed away and
shrank into a corner, head down and tail down. My
friend, easily stirred to pity and always interested in
the odd man out, went over to this puppy. He
promptly cowered lower and trembled when she
put out her hand to stroke him and pick him up. 'I
must have this one' she thought – and said.
Apparently this particular puppy appealed to her
maternal instinct and also presented a challenge.
She pictured him gradually gaining confidence and,
little by little, substituting affection for fear and joy
for doubt. Her choice turned out to be a big
mistake!

Hamish, as she named him, grew up to be a
genuine problem-dog. He was jumpy with her
human friends and, with other dogs, he alternated
unpredictably between terror and unprovoked
aggression. The link, in all species, between fear and
pugnacity is well-known but it was more than that
with Hamish. A wild, glazed, unseeing look would
come into his eye and then one gained the
impression that he literally did not know what he
was doing; he completely lost control – of his own
wishes as well as those of his distressed owner. On
these occasions he looked temporarily insane. The
human race is not unique in producing psychotics.

Hamish's difficulties were not confined to social
situations. His appetite was capricious: he was
always fussy about his food and sometimes he
refused to eat – in which event his mistress would
prepare a different meal and offer it to him, morsel
by morsel, in her fingers. Such treatment is
inadvisable with pets, since it is liable to create a

vicious spiral, and – in the absence or illness of his owner – the dog may actually starve himself to death. A dog manifesting such behaviour is a tremendous tie. He is not welcome in other people's houses, even in the houses of dog-lovers; he does not thrive in kennels; and, understandably, it is hard to find someone who is willing to dog-sit for a day or two.

Hamish remained a difficult feeder all his life. In addition, he was dangerous with strangers and even with his owner's friends. He would suddenly attack their feet as they walked into a room, his teeth sinking into their shoes – and, sometimes, getting through soft suede or canvas, to their socks, tights or skin! That his behaviour was due to 'nerves' rather than to malice did not render it more acceptable – or easier to modify. He would sometimes snap unexpectedly at even his nearest and dearest.

He would spend quite a lot of time hiding under pieces of furniture and refusing to come out – even at the prospect of a walk. The latter conduct is not unusual in a normal dog during, for instance, a thunder-storm, or a firework display (many animals react fearfully to loud, inexplicable noises or to electricity in the air), but Hamish would dive under a bed or a chest-of-drawers for no reason at all. He also had a disconcerting habit of cowering under stationary cars, refusing to emerge and snapping at any encouraging hand.

Thus Hamish has taught us two lessons: first that an initial meeting with a puppy can tell us a good deal about his future personality. A timid, trembling, mistrustful puppy is a less good bet than is his friendly, extraverted, forthcoming sibling. It is harder to assess mature dogs since these are not naturally as playful and optimistic as are run-of-the-mill puppies who have been well-treated. It is noteworthy, however, that dogs who have enjoyed a happy puppyhood and adolescence remain more 'puppyish' than dogs who have been largely ignored or treated inconsistently or beaten into submission. Happy dogs will often continue to enjoy rough-and-tumble games, such as ball-catching, tail-chasing and fence-jumping, long after they have reached physical maturity, i.e. at 18 months to two years. Some retain these habits until they attain ten years or so.

Hamish teaches us a second lesson in the way he exemplifies pathological symptoms. It is not normal for a dog to hide under furniture – unless he has a guilty conscience and is seeking to evade retribution or, as suggested earlier, is frightened for instance of a thunder-storm. If a dog has a habit of plunging under a bench or table for no apparent reason – and snarling threateningly at your efforts to entice him out – all is not well with him. Again, if he snaps at people he knows and habitually likes, this is pathological. If he actually bites somebody, breaking the skin or tearing a garment, the victim has the right to appeal to the police. In Britain a dog is legally allowed one bite and one bite only.

Shrinking and cowering are further danger-signals – unless of course the dog is frequently beaten or kicked, in which event such behaviour is to be expected. But this book is not intended for dog-owners of this kind. Puppies are both easily frightened and usually anxious to please. They should be treated firmly but kindly and patiently, if they are to grow up stable, cheerful and obedient.

Some puppies – and some adult dogs – suffer from convulsions or fits. These are characterised by jerky, convulsive, uncontrolled movements; there may be foaming at the mouth; and a glazed, unseeing look is observable in their eyes, if these are open. Such animals are often extra sensitive and require specially careful handling. The vet. should be consulted: it is sometimes possible to control the fits by drug therapy. If the dog does not grow out of these fits within a few months, it is probably wise to have him put down. In this event take him to the vet. yourself: the dog will have your moral support to the end and you will have seen for yourself that he died swiftly and painlessly.

This is the best thing to do, also, with a dog who, like Hamish, persistently displays dangerous, neurotic or inexplicably moody behaviour. If the dog is depressed and unpredictable it is kinder to him – as well as to your friends and yourself – to get the vet. to put him down than to continue the long struggle, year after year, with no hope of improvement.

A last word on the question of pathological behaviour in the dog. The word behaviour suggests something observable, objective, perhaps even measurable. This is how the term is used by 'behavioural scientists'. But I have several times referred to the expression on a dog's face, particularly in his eyes. Nobody would deny the expressiveness of the human face – though this is not wholly objective. Two observers may interpret the expression on a third person's face quite differently and, on stage or film, different actors will produce similar effect by using quite different facial techniques.

It is not surprising that dogs in constant contact with responsive humans should have recognisable facial expressions. What *is* surprising, however, is the frequency with which people will deny that dogs (and other animals) can and do smile or sulk or plead by means of their eyes, ears and tilt of head. Such people may well fail to notice if a dog is expressing suspicion or pain or loss of control; and they may well voice astonishment at the responsive, co-operative behaviour of a dog who has been trained carefully, treated consistently and understood throughout his life.

CHAPTER 5

Working Dogs

In the earlier chapters I have given an account of the general behaviour of dogs. These were written primarily for the pet-dog owner; hence their descriptions of normal and not-so-normal canine conduct in the home. But a true understanding of dogs' behaviour must be based on other contexts as well as the home. With this in mind I have selected (a) three types of well established working dogs – who work with the police, with shepherds and with the blind; (b) one relatively new type of working dog – whose task is to help the deaf; and (c) a vaguer, more controversial function, at which dogs have proved themselves particularly effective, namely as therapists with disturbed and handicapped people, and also with the old and lonely. I describe in detail the selection, training and experience of these working dogs in the following chapters.

People are generally fascinated by the ability of working dogs – their co-operativeness, adaptability, concentration and sense of responsibility. Even those who deprecate the notion of a dog being able to think and who disparage the relationship between loving owner and pet dog as sentimental – even they have, reluctantly, to admit the usefulness and resourcefulness of the sheep dog and the guide dog. 'Well, they're different', they say vaguely or 'Well, they're necessary' or even, unblushingly,

'Well, *they're* wonderful', as though such dogs were another species.

The dog-owner can learn a great deal from working dogs and their handling, about the dog's potential for intelligent behaviour. These different kinds of work illustrate the kind of behaviour of which many dogs are capable given suitable training. The chapters on working dogs suggest the age at which to begin basic training (a few weeks old) and the methods (little and often) to employ as well as the ages at which advanced training may be started – varying, to some extent, with the breed and the individual. Many pet owners will not want to go beyond the basic training stage. But the point is that training your dog or puppy, and understanding his behaviour, are intimately related. The two go forward together, you and the dog gaining in mutual understanding as training proceeds. One of the most striking features in the selection of working dogs is the emphasis placed on heredity. With police dogs, sheep dogs and guide dogs for the blind, it is an observed fact that the offspring bred 'to measure' consistently do better than those of unknown, or less highly selected, parents; and that the descendants of outstanding ancestors tend to become the future stars – in whatever sphere. The dangers of over-much inbreeding are well known and it is wise to call in new blood periodically. But once the requisite physical and mental features have been recognised, they can be bred for to an impressive extent.

Excellent puppies develop into excellent adult dogs, provided they receive appropriate training, at an appropriate stage. It may be recalled that early environment was stressed just as much as the genetic element. Neither breeding alone, nor training alone, is the answer. With canines as with humans, the *interaction* of nature and nurture is all-important, neither one being separable in practice from the other.

A further feature common to the training tactics of police-, sheep-, guide-dog and hearing-dog handlers is the constant meting out of praise during instruction and the avoidance of administering any form of punishment. During the days that I spent at the Training Establishments and field trials and exercises, observing dogs-with-handlers and listening to instructors, I never saw a blow given or heard a harsh word. This certainly had nothing to do with my presence! Almost every instructor with whom I spoke volunteered that his method of training depended on rewarding desired behaviour, with a caress or a word of commendation; and the most frequent advice I heard given to the blind students was along the lines of '*Good* girl! – *Tell* her she's a good girl!'

Several handlers elaborated on this theme to me. 'The dogs are willing, you see – they'd have been weeded out before now if they were lazy or stupid or stubborn. They want to please, they're doing their best – so we praise them when they get it right. If they get it wrong, well, we try again. They've got a lot to learn and they need encouragement. They mustn't lose confidence.'

A further feature in common was the vigorous health of the dogs, whatever their job. Whilst it is true that they are exceptionally well cared for physically – good diet and plentiful exercise – my impression was that the dogs are well, largely because they enjoy the one-to-one relationship with their owners, they know what is required of them and they like their work. In a word, these working dogs are never *bored*: they spend their time either working or enjoying well-earned rest. Quite a lot of pet dogs suffer from boredom – either because they spend too much of the day alone or because they have 'nothing to do' even when with their owner. A pet needs to be talked to and played with from time to time, just as a child does: otherwise he tends to get bored, resulting perhaps in destructiveness or lethargy – or indifferent health. Such tendencies do not occur with the working dog. Incidentally, despite the one-to-one relationship, most working dogs are friendly and tolerant of other members of the family and of strangers. Police dogs and guide dogs are bred to this and trained to it.

When the police dog or guide dog is off duty, however, he becomes a pet dog. (This is not true in general of sheep dogs, who usually sleep and live out in a barn or a shed when they are off duty. But sometimes the farmer's children grow very fond of the sheep dogs.) The guide dog knows exactly when he goes on and off duty because of his uniform – his harness. As soon as this is removed he shrugs off his responsibilities and relaxes – enjoying the companionship of his owner but no longer feeling in charge of him. Hearing dogs for the deaf are on duty virtually 24 hours a day but their work is less concentrated and onerous than is that of the guide dog.

The chapter on guide dogs for the blind is considerably longer than the other three chapters on working dogs. This is because there are, in effect, three lots of instruction involved in the training of guide dogs. The policeman has his dog allocated to him and *he* then becomes the dog-handler; the sheep farmer usually trains his own Border Collie(s); the hearing dog is 'trained to measure' by a professional handler and then introduced to his owner. But at the Centre for Guide Dogs, first the trainees have the courses of lectures and reading and practice which turns them – after some three years – into qualified instructors. Secondly, the *dogs* have to receive their basic training, working for months with handlers at the Centre. And, finally, there is the month's intensive training of guide-dog-plus-blind-owner. During his year of training, the guide dog is being prepared for a completely new life, in a completely new environment. Hence it is not surprising that that chapter has greater length and density than the other three.

A difference between the sheep dog, on the one hand, and the other three workers on the other, is that *instinct* probably plays a larger role in the work of the sheep dog than it does in any of the others. Many dogs naturally 'round up' moving objects – whether these be sheep, cattle, geese or human beings – and the Border Collie is particularly prone to rounding up, even without training. If a pet Collie (Border or Sheltie or 'Lassie' type) is taken for a country walk by several people and these separate into, say, two smaller groups, the dog is liable to run continuously from one group to the other, patently trying to get them to rejoin, and sometimes even evincing signs of distress if they fail to do so.

I designate this as instinctive because it is untaught, it appears at quite an early age and it is common to a great many members of the breed. Whilst it is true that the training of police dogs, guide dogs and hearing dogs also capitalises to some extent on their innate traits, my impression is that many of their tasks build less on instinct than is the case with sheep dogs.

Can any parallels be drawn between working dogs and human beings? I think that one or two can be drawn – that are not immediately obvious to people who have not pondered the question, and not at all obvious to those who dismiss dogs, along with cats, monkeys, horses and birds, as 'lower animals' and, hence, virtually incapable of thought or feeling. The working dog resembles the working person in being more cheerful, more fulfilled and possessing more self-esteem than the unemployed. Among un-employed dogs I would include pets who are ignored or neglected or over-pampered as well as stray dogs and those that have been deliberately exiled from their homes (dumped on a motorway, for instance, or abandoned in a forest – or simply left uncared-for when the family goes away).

If I am right in this, the dog resembles man in that having a job suits him, but the dog tends to revel in his work in a way that many human beings do not. On the other hand, it must be remembered that the working dog is specially selected and trained for his particular work, whereas many employed men and women find themselves in jobs that they are unfitted for and do not like.

Finally, dogs tend to have a single-mindedness and enthusiastic, long-lasting loyalty to job and companion that is comparatively rare in humans. This is not simply because the average dog is basically a kinder, less selfish creature than the average person. It is largely because the dog is less complex and less evolved than the human being. He is not beset by ambitions, assailed by advertise-ments, challenged by competition, torn by con-flicts, troubled by creative urges and overtaken by technology as we are; nor is he as naturally sadistic and frequently guilt-ridden as man. Humans are apt to render themselves needlessly frustrated and miserable: but if a dog is frustrated and miserable, this is generally due to our treatment of him.

CHAPTER 6

Police Dogs

Police dogs are such a familiar sight that it is surprising to learn that their large-scale use by the Police Force dates only from the 1940s. In the preceding decades a few guard dogs were used in the British Army and some dog patrols were employed in Europe, notably in Germany, but – although the Home Office set up a committee in 1934 to consider the whole issue – the police did not welcome the idea at that time. They feared that the dogs might prove dangerous and that their use might adversely affect police relations with the public. In 1939, with the outbreak of World War II, all trials and research on the topic ceased.

In the mid-1940s, interest was renewed and the Police Force now employs several hundred dogs. The training – of each dog and his handler – is long and intensive and their jobs are very varied. These comprise tracking – which may concern a criminal, a lost child, an adult with memory-loss or the recovery of property; the 'chase and stand-off', in which a police dog helps to apprehend an offender of some sort; searching for an object – which may be as large as a car or as small as a wedding ring; and retrieving. 'Specialist dogs' are also employed to detect drugs and bombs.

The tasks may have to be carried out in sunlight, darkness or dusk – affecting, of course, the efficiency of the dog's vision; in wet, dry, misty or frosty weather – affecting the strength and quality of the relevant scent. A warm, humid atmosphere yields the most satisfactory scent. The dog's work may involve overcoming physical obstacles, such as high walls, locked gates, wide rivers or making way through tunnels (contrary to the instincts of many large dogs). Moreover in the course of his work the dog may encounter the sharp sound of a pistol-shot at short range or, indeed, the sting of a bullet, or a knife or stick wielded by someone ruthless and desperate.

Mutual trust, therefore, is essential between the dog and his handler. Each must know that he can place complete reliance on his partner: that neither will ever let the other down, no matter how unforeseen and demanding the situation. Thus the dog must be one hundred per cent obedient by the end of his training. He must know exactly what his handler requires of him whenever he is on duty and he must comply immediately. In addition to obedience, however, the dog requires sensitivity and courage – a rare combination – and he needs too to be quick on the uptake, equable in temperament, adaptable and resourceful, for no two emergencies are identical. Equally important is fine physique: he must be big and powerfully-built, swift, agile and enjoy excellent health.

What dogs possess this group of qualities – intelligence, guts, strength, speed and adaptability? Before discussing the various breeds, it must be stressed that every dog is an individual, as is every human being: generalising should therefore be done with caution. Certain breeds are clearly unsuitable as potential police dogs because they lack the size or weight, or are slow movers, or because they tend to be 'flighty' or over-excitable. The most overall useful breed of police dog is the Alsatian (or German Shepherd), but successes are found too among Labradors, Weimeraners, Dobermanns, Boxers, Airedales, Bouviers de Flandres and Rottweilers.

By no means every member of these breeds will make the grade. A few begin well but lack the staying-power or the concentration, others turn out to be wilful or aggressive or, on the contrary, too soft; yet others cannot cope with the crowds or the noise or the traffic that often go with the job; and some fail to achieve the mutual rapport with their handler. This is sometimes due to the dog and sometimes to the handler. In any partnership there has to be give-and-take, and the interaction of personalities is not always easy to foresee.

One reason why the Alsatian takes pride of place in this realm is because of his public image. The police dog need not be aggressive or vicious – indeed he *should not* be so – but the law-abider, like the wrong-doer, must respect him and stand somewhat in awe of him, as one who helps to enforce the law. The Alsatian has a reputation as a one-man-dog who allows no liberties to be taken with him and, for this reason, he has a head-start over most other breeds – with the possible exception of the Dobermann. For these reasons, the selection of the dogs is taken just as seriously as their training. The Police are occasionally offered a dog, as a gift or for purchase, by people unable to keep their dog and wishing to ensure a good life for it. A police dog's lot is indeed a happy one for he is assured of constant affection, exercise, grooming, generous and appropriate diet and – if he makes the grade – congenial work until retirement. Most working dogs actually *enjoy* their job.

9. Training police dogs: climbing a high wall.

10. Training police dogs: finding a hidden object.

For a dog to be worth consideration he will usually be between six and eighteen months old and be one of the breeds mentioned above. In the first instance, he will be examined in the home of his owner by an experienced 'dog sergeant'. If the latter considers the dog suitable, he is brought to the Dog Training Establishment for a period of two to three weeks – or sometimes less – and kept in a separate block of kennels. The dog will be groomed and walked by the kennel staff and, once he settles down, an instructor will test the dog's behaviour in crowded shopping areas, will test him on the training field with other dogs and observe his reaction to the sound of close gunfire. If the dog is found to possess the requisite qualities, he is allocated to a handler and training is begun in the usual way. The preliminary tests are so stringent that few dogs fail to complete their training once they are accepted. But only about one in ten of the dogs offered to the Police Force do make the grade.

The majority of the satisfactory dogs are second, third or fourth generation police dogs, bred from known bitches and sires who have proved their worth. The Metropolitan Police have been breeding their own dogs since 1960, and a far higher proportion of these dogs successfully complete the course. During whelping the bitches and their puppies are cared for in the modern breeding block at the main Dog Training Establishment. Thus both the heredity and the environment of these future police dogs are known and are controlled – though even here, not every puppy does graduate. The Police usually find good homes for dogs that fail at some stage of their training.

Bitches and male dogs are employed as police dogs and both prove equally effective. The bitches

11. *Training police dogs: carrying an object.*

are spayed at about two years of age if they are not going to be bred from, but the dogs are very seldom castrated – and only on veterinary advice. Thus dogs of both sexes live and train in close proximity, yet – so intensive is the training and so keen are the dogs on their work – that sex is very rarely a problem. Equally impressive is the control the dogs learn to exert on that other universal instinct – excretion. When I visited the Police Dog Training Establishment, I spent about two hours watching the dogs rehearsing for a display and others being walked by their civilian exercisers, but throughout this time I did not see a single dog urinate or defecate. I was told that they gradually learn to confine these functions to early morning and last thing at night; and that this was not the result of specific training but that the dogs come to adopt the habit of their own volition.

The selection of dog-handlers is as important as the selection of the dogs, and care is taken in the matching of handler to dog. The number of handler-applicants always exceeds the number of vacancies. In the past, all handlers were men, but recently a few women have been trained as handlers and, in view of their success, the proportion of women dog-handlers is likely to increase. All applicants to become dog-handlers are experienced policemen/women, having had several years on the beat and on other duties. Their record is considered, they are interviewed and their home is visited. A stable, harmonious home-background is desirable and it is preferred if the would-be handler is married. The wife too is interviewed and if she appears unwelcoming or unsympathetic towards dogs, the couple will not be accepted – for the police dog lives in his handler's home, when he is not on duty, and also after his retirement, usually at eight or nine years of age.

The puppy goes to live in his new home when he is three months old and, during the subsequent few months, he is taught the skills that every house-dog should learn: house-training, sitting on command, not rushing for his food, fetching and dropping a toy on command. He is taught too to get used to children, crowds, noise and traffic and to walk on the lead without pulling. During this period his temperament is keenly observed: ideally it will be steady and equable – neither over-excitable nor placid to the point of lethargy. Once a month the puppy and his handler attend the Dog Training Establishment for a check on its progress, both physical and mental, and the handler receives advice on training and any problems that may have arisen.

At nine months of age, dog and handler (by now good friends) return to headquarters for 'a week's training in basic obedience and nosework' and the early stages of police dog training are introduced. At twelve months plus, dog-and-handler go on a training course for 12-14 weeks. The dog is taught to track following a ground scent, to search different types of places such as open country, wooded areas and buildings for criminals or property, and to give tongue, or 'speak', as soon as he finds what he has been seeking. He is also taught to chase and hold criminals, but he is trained not to bite them. After this initial course a dog starts work on the District to which he is posted, but with his handler he is required to attend regular refresher courses.

This basic training includes several points of interest. First is the variety of the places in which the police dog must feel at home (unfamiliar

12. *Training police dogs: jumping a hurdle.*

buildings, woods and open country) and the diversity of jobs (searching for property of various kinds or for a particular person). Secondly, the teaching of a dog to 'speak': some dogs bark spontaneously far more frequently than others. It is easy to reward, and hence encourage, a dog for giving tongue – with a caress or a word of praise – but it is not so easy to instruct a naturally silent dog to speak on command. All police dog training, incidentally, is done by means of praise and encouragement: no beating or punishment is employed. At a later stage of training the dog has also to be trained to stay quiet, on command. There are crises in a policeman's life when the maintenance of silence is absolutely crucial. This can be a difficult skill to impart – particularly with a dog whom it has been hard to train to 'speak'.

A third point of interest is the training of the dog to 'chase and hold' a criminal but not to bite. All the instructors with whom I spoke emphasised the importance of never allowing the dog to injure anyone – for they are answerable to Parliament and the public, as I was reminded. Some dogs, I was told, who were shaping well, eventually failed because they became over-wrought and aggressive in moments of stress. The dog is trained to pursue a running figure (indicated by the handler) and, having caught up with the runner, it is the dog's task to leap up at the runner's right arm – or, rather, sleeve – and, hanging on to it, bring the person to the ground. The dog then retains his hold until the handler catches up and tells him to go. Practising this skill takes place with a volunteer who can run fast and who wears a jacket with a padded right-hand sleeve. The right arm is chosen because the majority of people are right-handed and the dog, in

13. *Training police dogs: apprehending a 'criminal'.*

14. *Training police dogs: walking down a ladder.*

addition to detaining the offender, may thus be able to deter him from shooting or stabbing.

Although police dogs are trained *not* to injure anyone and in fact they very seldom do so, the mere presence of the dog is salutory – many tough characters apparently shouting, panic-stricken, to the police, 'Call your dog off, for God's sake!' Their fear of the dog is greater than their fear of the policeman.

The police dog is, in general, an exceptionally happy, well-balanced creature, with glossy coat, bright eyes, impressive musculature, beautifully co-ordinated movements, his whole bearing radiating alertness and eagerness to help. When he reaches retirement age, he goes to live his declining years with his 'family' – with whom he has kept in touch throughout his working life. He continues to be treated with respect and affection and, although henceforth his life lacks the excitements to which he was accustomed, he settles down in old age and becomes guide, protector and friend to the family he has known from puppyhood.

CHAPTER 7

Sheep Dogs

Many people will have seen a sheep dog in action and some will have ventured out into the hills of Scotland or Wales or the flatter country of South and East England, to watch sheep dog trials and competitions in the wind and rain or – if they are fortunate – in bright sunshine. They observe that the dogs are, almost without exception, Border Collies and that for the most part the dogs appear to have remarkable control over the sheep in their charge.

Spectators marvel at the understanding, zeal, concentration and persistence of the dogs, at their selfless expenditure of energy, their good humour and their sagacity – expressed, for instance, in their care not to rush the sheep, their accurate grasping of what it is that the shepherd requires and their anticipation of occasional lapses on the part of the sheep. But the casual onlooker has, of course, little idea how this performance is achieved; they find the spoken or whistled commands of the handler – who may be hundreds of yards away or on the far side of a hill – quite baffling; and they may not realise the amount of time, skill and patience involved in attaining the harmonious partnership between man and dog. Moreover, it may not occur to the spectator that (even when he sees dogs scoring poorly) he is witnessing the exclusive top class – the few sheep dogs who make the highest grade. For every dog who reaches championship trials, there are dozens who have failed and will never succeed.

An observation made to me by the Secretary of the International Sheep Dog Society, was 'Most dogs are average and they find a niche' – i.e. they do useful work with sheep (and cattle) as farm dogs. On the other hand, as one expert shepherd told me, many of these average dogs might well have become champions had they been trained by one of the top handlers. Having now had the opportunity of watching sheep dogs and their handlers at every level from novices and nursery trials to supreme champions – I find this comment wholly convincing. Interestingly enough, the uninitiated (such as myself) learn most from watching the *less* expert dogs at work with the sheep. This is so, partly because one then realises that much that is taken for granted in the higher echelons – such as keeping the sheep together in a tightly-knit group – far from happening automatically, is in fact the result of long, patient training; and partly because one then has the opportunity of observing errors on the part of the handlers, themselves.

In this chapter I attempt to describe the methods of training by which the handler/sheep dog partnership is built up. Most Border Collies are innately intelligent; they possess a strong herding instinct and eager willingness to please; and for many generations these particular dogs have been bred for these traits. They are *not* bred for appearance – as are the dogs shown at Crufts'. Border Collies come in a variety of shapes, colours and coats. The classical Border Collie is mainly black with white paws, chest and tail-tip, and he characteristically has a white patch around his black nose; his eyes are dark brown, his coat longish and fairly fine, and his ears are dropped (like those of an Alsatian puppy during its first few months). But some highly successful working Border Collies have white in different places, whilst others are all black; a few are mainly 'red' – a warm, reddish-brown; some have pale eyes and some are prick-eared. Some are long-coated and some are smooth-coated – the latter being preferred, for obvious reasons, in hot climates and where there is a great deal of bracken.

Any combination of these points can be found, and none is remotely related to the dog's aptitude and trainability. The International Sheep Dog Society, being well aware of this fact and of the tendency of the Kennel Club to encourage breeding for looks only – and arbitrarily selected looks, at that – for long declined the invitation to include a class of Border Collie in the annual Dog Show. In 1976 they relented – on condition that working capacity should also be taken into account; and in 1982 appropriate working tests were devised by the International Sheep Dog Society, to be judged by two members of the International Panel.

It is clear that the Border Collie has great natural ability for work with sheep and, over the years, the most successful workers of both sexes have been bred from. The Supreme Championship Sheep Dog trials were inaugurated in 1906, and won by a dog called Don (registration No. 11, owned by R. Sandilands). Don was a descendant of Hemp (registration No. 9). Hemp was bred by Adam Telfer and was born in September 1893 and died in May 1901. Every Supreme Champion, since then, has been a descendant of Hemp's.

Without the training, however, the dogs would not be anything like as helpful to the sheep-farmer as they now are – enabling him to round up hundreds of scattered sheep in a few minutes; to segregate a given few who need special attention; to pen those requiring to be penned; and to seek out the occasional sheep or lamb that is ill or injured or heavily pregnant, or buried in snow, or has fallen into a ditch from which it is unable to extricate itself.

The puppies live in the house until their serious training is begun. In these early days they learn the general attitude of obedience and, in particular, to lie down, to walk on and to stop, when ordered. The handler generally embarks on the training, using a very long cord at first, when the dog is 8-12 months old and, in the early stages, training should be little and often (like feeding puppies), as a sheep-farmer commented to me. A few trainers like to start earlier but the general feeling is that a younger puppy lacks the physical stamina and may not yet possess the requisite powers of concentration; also, very young puppies are easily scared and are apt to be impetuous. It is felt, too, that a young puppy may develop bad habits – and it is certainly harder to eradicate a bad habit than to inculcate a desirable one from the beginning. It is possible for a skilled handler to start training a dog which is over 18 months – or even, in some cases, over 2-$2\frac{1}{2}$ years – but this tends to be more difficult, especially if the dog has not received early lessons in elementary obedience. He may well take longer to train and his working life will of course be proportionally shorter.

The life of a working sheep dog is usually about 11-13 years. If he has a very tough assignment in the

15. *Sheep dog showing characteristic 'creeping' movement.*

16. *Sheep dog rounding up a flock.*

hills, covering 25-30 miles in a day, up hill and down
dale, it may be as short as 8-10 years. Unlike police
dogs, sheep dogs are not retired in old age. I am told
that they usually work for the whole of their
lifetime and that they prefer it that way. 'You try
and leave them at home – they bring the place
down!' From the age of nine or ten they tend to slow
up and their keen vision and hearing gradually
diminish. Round about this age, a thoughtful
sheep-farmer will put his dog on to the lighter jobs,
requiring him to cover less ground and to move less
swiftly. An experienced sheep dog is versatile and he
accepts whatever jobs are assigned to him. Some hill
dogs, after years of heavy work, are sold or given to
lowland (parkland) farmers, where they continue to
lead a useful, but physically less demanding life.

How then does the dog learn to carry out his
various tasks? What does the training consist of? I
was fortunate enough to be able to have a long talk
with Mr Norman Seamark, owner of a big sheep-
farm, National Vice-President of the English
Section of the International Sheep Dog Society and
trainer of several champions. He also very generously gave me a demonstration with four of his
experienced dogs working with some 300 sheep in a
30-acre field. He demonstrated how they would
work singly or in pairs, or all four co-operatively,
according to his commands. He had trained each
dog to respond to its own particular set of whistles –
which he produced by means of mouth-plus-fingers.

The dogs understood also his spoken commands
but, hearing words, they would not know which
command was meant for which dog. He has
perfected a one-to-one understanding between
himself and each dog, by the expedient of varying
the pitch, length, timbre and number of whistles.

Each dog responds to his own code and to no other – though the whistled command to stop is the same for all his dogs. One of the four was a bitch, and the other three were male – on which topic more below.

I duly watched these dogs racing away in a wide sweep to the far end to gather the sheep which were placidly grazing all over the field. The dogs never went very close to their charges, and they reduced their speed once they had reached the far end of the field, and had assembled them into one large group. In what seemed less than two minutes, the sheep were all confined in one corner of the field, near where we were standing in wind-swept rain. We stood still and the sheep took no notice of us, some passing within about a foot of us. They likewise ignored one of the four dogs who was obediently lying down between us and the relevant corner: in fact, they trotted into the corner, just avoiding treading on him. He remained motionless, as though oblivious of the sheep, although he was by this time entirely surrounded and hemmed in by them.

Later Mr Seamark demonstrated how the dogs would bring him sheep, as requested, from various directions and also how the dogs would drive the sheep away from him (one of the hardest tasks to teach); how the dogs would induce their charges to do a kind of slalom – officially called 'threading'; and how, when the sheep were standing facing one way by a fence, the dog would – when so ordered – bring back the sheep by slipping between them and the fence and turning them round.

He also described the kinds of tasks required of sheep dogs when entering competitions. These include getting a few sheep into single file; 'shedding' i.e. isolating one or more designated sheep from their fellows; and driving sheep between a couple of children, picked at random from the spectators, and placed on the ground a yard or two apart. These children were always, of course, unfamiliar to the dog – who ignored them as persons, since he was concentrating on the sheep.

I asked how it was possible to get the dogs to perform such complex and varied feats and was told that all their training is based on five simple commands:

(a) Go *left*, that is, to approach the sheep from the left, thus driving them towards the right. The phrase used for this command is 'Come by'.

(b) Go *right* – thus driving the sheep towards the left. The phrase for this is 'Away here'. Mr Seamark explained that at the start of this training, he always observed which side the dog naturally favoured and taught that particular command first. Thus if the dog was moving leftwards, he would say 'Come by' at this early stage, whereas if the dog was moving rightwards, he would say 'Away here', reinforcing whatever the dog had begun doing. He commented, in passing, that although *facing* the sheep and the dog, one must take care to issue the order consistently *from the dog's point of view*.

(c) Move *forward*, towards the sheep: 'Walk on'.

(d) 'Lie down' – self-explanatory.

(e) 'That'll do' – i.e. the exercise is ended.

In some cases, arm-signals are also used – where the terrain permits. But, as Mr Clark explained to me, this practice is frowned upon in some quarters since it necessitates the dog's momentarily taking his eyes off the sheep, thus risking decrease of control. According to many sheep dog handlers, the dog should *never* take his eyes off the sheep when he is driving them: 'One glance elsewhere' I was told, 'and he loses his contact with the sheep'. The hardest thing to teach a dog to do is *to leave* his sheep. He knows he is in charge of them and he develops a strong sense of responsibility towards them.

The five commands are universal among British shepherds and trainers – 'though they'll say it in Welsh, in Wales' I was told. When a trained sheep dog is sold abroad to a non-English-speaking country, a tape is often made for the benefit of the new owner – who learns his part by listening to the cassette. He has to learn to imitate the sounds and to teach the dog to get used to his voice, habits and personality. The British sheep dog is quite an important export, to countries all over the world.

In general, when the dog has acquired the five basic skills, his handler gradually accustoms him to working to a whistle, instead of to a voice. The whistle may be 'just a piece of tin' as an ex-shepherd from Dorset explained to me – 'but it gives a wide range of sounds' – or it may be plastic or, as is the case with Mr Seamark, the sounds may be produced simply by lips, fingers and air. Whistles are preferable to the spoken word because their sound carries further – crucial on large farms, in hilly country and in windy weather – and they offer a wider range of pitch, thus enabling the handler to control several sheep dogs simultaneously. With experience, each dog comes to recognise its own set of whistles: Nick ignores the command given to Meg to go left but as soon as he hears the order specific to him, to go right he obeys it (and of course Meg ignores this). Each handler evolves his own 'whistle code'.

It is now clear that the process of producing a well-trained, experienced canine partner in this sphere is long and arduous – but extremely rewarding. All the handlers with whom I talked remarked that partnership is indeed the correct term but they always added that the dog achieved results with an efficiency and promptness that they (the handlers) could not possibly manage on their own. They emphasised that the dog could cover the ground and get the sheep where required in an amazingly short time and that they were wholly dependent on the co-operation of their dogs. They also stressed, as the police had done, that there are immense individual differences among the dogs: that each is an individual in his own right and no two dogs are identical in temperament, talent or rate of development. These great differences obtain even among dogs of the same litter.

Once the dog has mastered the five basic skills, he begins to realise the ultimate aim of the instructions: *why* this command is given, *where* the handler wishes *which* sheep to go. Thus, the outstanding sheep dog after due experience on the farm and, perhaps, in trials, knows that the object of the exercise is to collect all members of the flock in the north-west corner or to herd a small group into a pen, etc. His obedience to his master never wavers but he may be observed to anticipate certain of the commands – and to counteract, of his own volition, an occasional misdemeanour on the part of a sheep.

I have heard it suggested that the highly specialised tasks demanded in the championship trials have little relevance to the day-to-day work of a dog on a sheep-farm, that the skill of controlling, say, 150 sheep at a time is very different from that of managing a mere handful of sheep (as is usually required in the trials) – and even that certain dogs are coached exclusively for trial work and would be of little use in an ordinary farming situation. This is evidently an issue on which the experts differ and I can claim no expertise in the matter. But I have been assured that such tactics are the exception rather than the rule; that controlling five or ten sheep, as opposed to one or two hundred, has its difficulties. 'In some ways it's easier to deal with a hundred. The handful of sheep get edgy and suspicious after a bit, in a way they don't do if they're with a big flock ... When they're brought away from home and in batches of five, they wonder what it's all about ... The two techniques are different, of course.'

It would appear that the tasks demanded of the dogs in the trials are indeed highly relevant. For instance, the separation of one sheep from its fellows may need to be done on the farm because the sheep has maggots or has gone lame or because it belongs to a neighbour. All the tasks required of sheep dogs in the trials are similar to jobs that need doing on the farm. The numbers are different, the locale and the noise-level are different, but the best dog will be he who embodies obedience, understanding and conscientiousness – with flexibility and unflappability.

The sheep used for the trials are mostly ewes. The majority of sheep dogs are male but there are a few working bitches and these are well spoken of. Those who reach competition level are said to do very well in the trials. As working dogs they are 'softer' in manner than the males, more propitiating and easier to handle. They are not spayed because a good bitch will be needed to breed from. The male is bigger and more powerful physically. If he is put off by working with a bitch who is in season, he is not an ideal sheep dog. The males are more aggressive and

17. *Sheep dog herding sheep into an enclosure.*

18. *Sheep dog 'holding' sheep.*

will sometimes attempt to dominate their handlers, if given the chance. They come into their own with belligerent sheep – who are not exclusively rams. Some even occasionally show pugnacious propensities and the Border Collie usually responds to belligerence by means of his 'strong eye'. This phrase, the 'eye' of the sheep dog was used repeatedly by my informants. It refers to a peculiarly concentrated, almost hypnotic expression in the eyes of the Border Collie and is unique to the breed. I was even told that a few dogs overdo the use of the eye! 'You can get excess of eye – just staring'.

However, controlling sheep by staring at them, then perhaps lying down and renewing the fixed, unwavering gaze, then rising again, is infinitely preferable to harrying the sheep – by nipping or 'gripping' them or going in too close, or rushing them. A dog that grips in the trials is usually penalised, i.e. he will lose points, but the judge will not necessarily disqualify him. If the dog dives in and grips without provocation, then he is disqualified: this, incidentally, is usually a sign of the dog's weakness. But if a stubborn ewe turns to face him and attempts to charge and he stands his ground and grips, very few judges would disqualify him for this behaviour. 'A dog that runs away from a difficult ewe is useless to someone who has a job of work to do. The trial field is supposed to be the proving ground for Sires and Dams of future working dogs. Hence a realistic attitude must be taken on this point – as on all others.' (Mr Seamark)

A *steady pace* when driving sheep is essential. 'If sheep are made to gallop, they'll never slow down' and 'you don't want to knock flesh off them'. Thus the *outrun* must be wide, sweeping and pear-shaped –

when the dogs go racing over the brow of the hill, or to the far end of the field, to gather their charges: in this way, when moving fast, the dogs do not approach too closely to the sheep and they collect any that are straying way out. Similarly the *lift* – when the dog has assembled all the sheep – should be gentle. One of the skills that the sheep dog must learn is that he is expected to lose no time over the outrun but that, once the sheep are within his control, he must move more slowly, maintaining his distance and being prepared to lie down – using the 'eye' – ready to rise swiftly but move circumspectly on command. Sheep must be moved at a controlled pace – something that is not always easy to grasp for the keen young sheep dog in training. They should not, however, be moved so slowly that they begin grazing.

Most sheep-farmers do their own dog-training and the technique is often passed on from father to son. But some lack the time or the patience and these will usually seek advice, or purchase partially trained dogs. The Agricultural Training Board runs courses for handlers; some Agricultural Colleges include sheep dog training among their courses; and there are many books on the subject. Some farmers, however, have been astonished when attending trials for the first time, to 'discover just what a sheep dog can do for you. A man just *couldn't do* the same job – even on a lowland farming field.' Some members of the International Sheep Dog Society concentrate wholly on breeding: they leave the task of training to others. The main function of the Society is to register the Border Collie puppies – some 6,500 a year – they hold records of the pedigree of every registered dog, these pedigrees going back fifty years. 'We have a responsibility to the breed', said the Secretary, 'Anything we can do to further the breed, we should do'. The Society also organises the trials 'but these are merely the shop-window'. On the other hand, the trials have intrinsic importance in that they highlight the remarkable ability of the best dogs – who are often selected to breed from and who account for a substantial number of exports. Moreover the fact that the tests used in the trials have scarcely changed over the decades is itself indicative of their value. They began in 1873 – at that time an informal half-day, with shepherds running their dogs in friendly rivalry.

The dogs taking part in the Supreme Championship trials are all born and trained in Britain (because of our quarantine laws) but the clientele – the watchers and would-be purchasers – are indeed international, coming from France, Switzerland, Germany, The Netherlands, Norway, South Africa, the U.S.A. and Canada.

A last word about the dogs themselves. The vast majority, as has been said, are Border Collies. They were evolved from cross-breeding 'rough collies – the Lassie type' – with Gordon Setters. Sometimes a trace of other breeds is suggested: perhaps some Whippet, some Labrador, possibly Borzoi, the Scotch Beardie, the Welsh Hillman. This is controversial and buried in the mists of time. Two points, however, are certain, namely that the word collie is Gaelic for 'useful' and that the old English Sheep Dog is no longer used as a farm worker. Mr Seamark told me that this dog used not to be so large, heavy and hairy: 'He wouldn't *see* a bullock now at about ten yards, with all that hair in his eyes!' The changes in his appearance are due once again to capricious, fickle fashion. The Bearded Collie, however, is still sometimes a useful sheep dog. One Beardie recently showed such outstanding working ability that he was officially registered by the Society.

It will be remembered that the other name for the Alsatian is German Shepherd, so I enquired about these dogs in this connection. I was told that in Biblical times, sheep dogs had above all to be guard dogs and even nowadays, in some countries, there are still predatory wolves. In that capacity the Alsatian can be very useful, said my informant (who knew, incidentally, of one particular Alsatian bitch who helped a farmer to gather his ewes) but in general they are said to lack 'the finesse and, especially the eye' for which the Border Collie is famous.

There is thus a good deal in common between the sheep dog and the police dog. In both cases a partnership based on mutual trust is built up between man and dog; each member of the pair relies upon the other and is happy to do so; the dog grows to understand his role, to enjoy it and to take pride in it. Apart from actually liking his work, he enjoys the physical exercise and the close personal relationship with his handler. These dogs are rarely unwell or moody, and never bored; in fact, their buoyant health and happiness are very striking.

CHAPTER 8

Guide Dogs for the Blind

The essential partnership between the policeman and his dog, and the shepherd and his dog, has been outlined. The relationship between the blind person and his guide dog, however, is more than a partnership: they operate *as a unit* rather than as two individuals with close rapport. Moreover the dependence of the blind on their guide dogs is sometimes literally a matter of life and death. Two examples will suffice to show that this is no overstatement. The dog who refuses to leave the pavement, when ordered forward by her owner to cross the road, is apt to be quite right: she senses a traffic danger of which her owner is unaware. Again the guide dog that disobeys her owner, who proposes to step out of a train – which, unbeknown to the blind man, has overshot the platform – is probably saving her owner from an accident, if not from death.

These incidents illustrate a further point peculiar to guide dogs for the blind. Unlike the implicit obedience noted in other working dogs, the guide dog has on occasion to make an independent decision and act on it – contrary to her owner's instructions. This capacity to take matters into her own paws and to refuse to carry out an order is an exceedingly interesting phenomenon, in view of the many months intensive training in obedience which guide dogs undergo. It indicates that the dog *understands* what is going on, she has learned to think for herself and think ahead, and she looks at the situation from the viewpoint of the blind person's well-being. Her training and experience have instilled a strong sense of responsibility and professionalism. When the guide dog is wearing her uniform, i.e. her specially designed harness, she is indeed a dedicated professional. When the harness is removed, she becomes a normal, carefree, fun-loving dog – enjoying the company of other people, other dogs and the free exercise that is prescribed for her.

How is this achieved? It is not due to some magic formula or innate sense of expedience. It is a long story, starting with the selection of suitable parents for a guide dog to-be; continuing through puppy-hood (the 'puppy-walking' stage) into young adulthood (the months of practice at one of the Training Centres run by the Association of Guide Dogs for the Blind) and culminating in the four weeks – still at the Training Centre – with the carefully matched blind owner-to-be. Throughout this period regular checks on the dog's physical and mental health are carried out and this caring vigilance is maintained after the dog has been taken over by her blind owner. Let us consider each stage in turn.

Selection The vast majority of guide dogs have been bred by the Association – which owns about 160 breeding bitches and some 35 stud dogs. Occasionally puppies are bought from reputable breeders, enabling the Association to assess stock from different strains and to add to their established breeding animals. Labradors, Golden Retrievers, Curly-coat Retrievers, Alsatians and crosses of these breeds are used most frequently. Labrador/ Golden Retriever crosses are especially successful; occasionally other breeds, such as Boxers and Collies, are considered. Dogs of these breeds are acquired from time to time as adult stock, aged ten months to $2\frac{1}{2}$ years.

Sixty to 65 per cent of guide dogs are bitches as they tend to be more biddable, less dominant than the males, and less easily distracted by other dogs when on duty. The remaining 35-40 per cent are males – castrated at the time when they first start cocking their leg to urinate. 'If they are castrated too early, it can create zombies – and if too late, it may be ineffectual', explained Mr Stephen Wright, Controller at the Leamington (oldest-established) Training Centre. The males become equally good guide dogs and, as they are in general larger and stronger, they are usually allocated to larger, more capable blind persons – not necessarily men.

The bitches are spayed after they have come into season once. As they exceed in number the guide dog males, the feminine pronoun 'she' is used throughout this chapter, when referring to the guide dogs. I shall continue to use the masculine pronoun 'he' for the owners and the trainers – although there the ratios are in fact 50/50.

An essential requirement in a guide dog is that she stands at least 19 inches to the shoulder, in order to ensure the necessary balance and momentum between dog-in-harness and owner. Some variation is of course required so that exceptionally tall or short person can be suited. But in general very big dogs are not wanted as they are more difficult to match, they are expensive to feed and 'they can't shove under a bus seat or be carried up an escalator.

We do sometimes take individuals of other breeds but we'd be unlikely to take an Old English Sheep Dog or a Standard Poodle because of all the grooming and clipping every so often.' In addition to height, the potential guide dog needs to be strong and well-built, to possess an excellent health-record and to have very acute hearing and vision.

Intelligence, conscientiousness and equable temperament are just as important as are the physical traits. Temperament was a word that cropped up repeatedly during my visit to the Guide Dog Training Centre. In this connection it concerns steadiness, alertness, tolerance, resilience and the right degree of body sensitivity. To quote from the Association's leaflet on *Training a Guide Dog*: 'Too high a sensitivity might cause a dog to jump at an unexpected pat, with perhaps disastrous results for its blind owner; whereas too low a sensitivity might cause it to take too many bumps and bruises. The guide dog is trained to treat the human being on the other end of the harness *as part of itself* [my italics] so that its reactions to obstacles and hazards extend to both of them'. Needless to say, the dog's emotional sensitivity is as important a factor as her body sensitivity. Again this should be neither too intense (allied as this sometimes is to timidity) nor too low (allied as this sometimes is to brashness).

These, then, are the qualities which are sought in the brood bitches and the stud dogs, and it is found that a high proportion of their progeny faithfully reproduce these physical and mental traits. The puppies remain with their mother until the age of about seven weeks, after which they are boarded out with their 'puppy-walking' family – usually consisting of parents and several children, living in a town

19. *Training a puppy as a guide dog.*

20. *Training a guide dog to negotiate obstacles.*

within 30 miles of the relevant Training Centre. Urban life is important as the puppy must get used to the noise, speed and bustle of cars, fire-engines, motor-cycles, road-works, etc; the hazards of shopping and travelling by public transport; the visits of tradesmen; the presence of strangers, cats, dogs and other household pets. It is desirable that the family includes children, so that the guide dog to-be learns to cope with them, but the person in full charge of the puppy is nearly always the Mother of the family.

Her title is the 'puppy-walker' but she under-takes to do a great deal more than walking the new member of the household. She looks after the puppy until she is ready to go to the Training Centre – at 10-14 months. During her year with the family, she is house-trained, inoculated, groomed regularly and taught the basic commands, *Sit, Come, Down* and *Stay*. The actual walking is crucial, however, as she must learn to walk in the centre of the pavement, on the left-hand side of her walker, not pulling, but slightly ahead – as she will have to do when trained as a guide dog.

At the end of this period she is assessed for her fitness as a guide dog – unless it has become evident, earlier, that she is unsuitable. Dogs may be found to fail at any stage in their training. 'The dog that makes *slow* progress is the heart-break' said Mr Wright, 'you keep on trying – and may not succeed in the end'. A dog may have to be rejected because it is too clinging or too independent. All rejected dogs are found a good home, either as a pet or as a worker. 'A dog with too much drive – a workaholic – might well go to the Police or to the R.A.F. as a search-dog.'

Training A dog's training at the Centre consists

of three stages: for the first three-five months she is a member of the Early Training Unit (E.T.U.). The Training Assistant's task here is to settle the dog down and to 'get her responsive; to stop her being distracted by other dogs and smells – and cats – and prepare her for her future work'. The training she received in her puppy-walking family will be consolidated and she will probably do a little kerb-work (learning to stop and sit), and learn about stairs and obstacle-avoidance and turning with her handler. She will be taken for 'incentive walks' to the park, which she enjoys. At first this is done using the lead, but after some weeks she is introduced to her harness which she wears and works in, for short periods. She continues, however, to have some practice on the lead, learning also to walk to heel on the lead, as her owner-to-be will in due course be holding a (loose) lead, as well as the harness-handle. Thus if he accidentally drops the harness he 'is not wholly lost' – as a blind owner put it to me.

The second stage lasts for a further twelve weeks. She now has to acquire the harder skills, i.e. obedience to instructions such as *right* and *left*, *forward* and *back*, *steps*, *find*. Moreover she has to learn that avoidance of obstacles includes her handler as well as herself; that an overhanging branch or a leaning ladder may obstruct her companion although she, herself, can easily pass underneath it; that an uneven surface or a hole in the road, is dangerous for her companion – who must be guided round it.

At this stage she is learning that she-plus-handler are effectively one unit, that she is the leader and protector as well as being an obedient servant. In a word, she is beginning to learn that her companion at the end of the harness is dependent on her. At a

21. *Training a guide dog – a puppy walker.*

later stage in the training, the instructor does actually go out with the dog, blindfold. In this way he learns her strengths and weaknesses and it also helps him to build up a picture of the sort of blind person whom she will suit and the sort of environment in which she will best be able to work.

The third stage is the vital month in which the dogs are introduced to their owners-to-be and during which the pairs learn to work (and play) together. But before going on to this, let us consider the selection and training of the instructors themselves.

Selection and Training of Instructors The Training Centres receive *two or three applications per day* for the post of training assistant; thus selection is a genuine problem. My informant categorised most applicants as primarily 'dog-people' or 'do-gooders' – the latter being over-full of pity for the blind. In his view the 'dog-people' are often better suited to the job. 'The blind don't want pity ... and you need someone who can be firm if necessary – who can learn to understand and train the dogs'.

The training of instructors is quite tough. It takes three years and 'they end with a semi-professional qualification ... All the expenses of their education are paid.' Normally they work a 9 – 5, five-day week but for a solid month, when practising dogs with students, they get only three half-days off and only two or three evenings a week. This means $10\frac{1}{2}$ days overtime during the month and it happens two or three times a year. This is a highly effective test of motivation. At the end of each of these periods the trainer gets five days off to recuperate.

The selected instructors are indeed strongly motivated from the beginning and they become wholly dedicated to the cause and to their particular dogs. 'The best instructors are "middle-of-the-road", gregarious types: they like people and animals and, very often, children. So it's almost like selecting for marriage!' commented Mr Wright with dry humour. In addition to these general characteristics, they need of course to love and understand dogs, to possess endless patience, acute powers of observation and a faculty of empathy – to be able to realise how it feels to be a dog in training and also how it feels to be a blind person faced with an unfamiliar sentient being – on whom he will be heavily dependent, yet who will be wholly dependent upon him.

Applicants often write at sixteen or seventeen but they are not accepted as trainers until they reach twenty years of age. At that age, some will have done the less stringent E.T.U. and these will know exactly what they are taking on. In addition to the daily routine of feeding, weighing, grooming, etc. – which includes inspecting ears and eyes and examining for parasites – and the general duties of practising the dog on the skills already described, there are a host of minute details whose importance must be grasped and which have to be meticulously attended to whenever the dog is wearing her harness. In due course, these must be communicated to the blind owner. They include correct positioning of feet, appropriate distancing from the dog while holding her harness-handle, suitable speed of movement and of balance between dog-plus-harness and handler, acceptable degree of tension – communicated through the harness.

22. *Training a guide dog – sitting at the kerb.*

Some of these points can be learned by rote, such as the positioning of the right foot slightly *behind* the left foot, when waiting at the kerb, ready to start off with the right foot. But others require delicate, sensitive adjustments for they concern matters of which the individual is unaware at first and which it is going to be tricky to convey to the blind owner-to-be. Like most skills, when it is well done it all looks easy and relaxed to the spectator. The onlooker does not see the best of this game unless he knows the rules and is adept at this particular activity himself.

The future dog owners Before the twelve blind persons arrive at the Training Centre, preliminary research on them is conducted. Not every blind man or woman is suitable to own a guide dog; if he has a serious loss of hearing or suffers from some major physical or mental disability, he is usually not accepted. Some people with residual sight are considered suitable but, interestingly enough, if someone has *too much* vision he may not make a good owner for a guide dog. For example he will dimly apprehend the presence of an obstacle – such as a tree or a letter-box – and he may elect to avoid it by going to the right of it. The dog, however, may have decided to take her owner to the left of the obstacle. In this event, dog and owner will either tumble over each other or they may start off in opposite directions – jarring each other unpleasantly. This kind of conflict will undermine the dog's confidence and will, in effect, 'untrain' her as Mr Wright put it.

Investigation of the suitability of the blind person as a potential guide dog owner begins with an interview based on a private and confidential all-inclusive Form, completed by an experienced member of the Training Centre. This covers the applicant's age, height, weight and build; his marital status, religion (for dietary reasons) and occupation. Related to occupation are questions such as whether the employer's permission has been obtained for the owner to have his dog at work. The future owner's type of living accommodation is also ascertained in order to determine whether a kennel and run for the dog will be required; whether fencing will be necessary; what relief facilities for the dog are available and what free running facilities there are. Many blind people live alone but, if the applicant is married and has children, the attitude of his family towards dogs is investigated, likewise the presence of other pets.

Then follow more psychological aspects such as the applicant's motivation for requesting a guide dog: Why is he applying just now? If registered as blind for more than three years, why hasn't he applied before? What changes does he anticipate a guide dog will bring to his life?

Detailed information about the applicant's hearing and residual vision, if any, is noted; and medical aspects are covered. The applicant is assessed on his traffic sense, his gait, posture and natural rate of walking, his talking voice and his speed of reaction; his previous experience with dogs – if any – is noted and his capacity to absorb and implement instruction is estimated. The last sheet of the interview questionnaire concerns the interviewer's summing-up and recommendation.

On the basis of the detailed record, the Controller of the Training Centre decides whether to accept the applicant and, in the event of acceptance (and when, after 12-18 months, he has reached the head of the queue), the decision is made which of the trained guide dogs to allocate to which 'students' – as accepted applicants are designated during their month of training.

The matching of dog to student is considered very important. Size and speed are obvious factors: a large, fast-moving dog will be allocated to a big student, probably male, with natural swiftness of movement. Some dogs, at the end of training, require more disciplining than others and this is taken into account when selecting their owner. 'The most demanding dogs go to the most capable people.' The dogs are trained to obey both voice and gestures, so a dog that responds particularly well to verbal orders will go to a student with a good voice. An owner who is slightly hard of hearing will need a dog with extra good hearing and alertness, in view of the hazards of traffic.

The owner's general life-style partly determines the type of dog he will receive. A woman in her 60s who rarely moves out of her home district, wanting a dog with which to do local shopping, to go to church and to visit her grandchildren, might do well with a small, rather clinging golden retriever bitch. Whereas a vigorous young man, constantly travelling around to new places, will want an energetic dog – perhaps a male Alsatian – that will enjoy the variety and exercise, and fit well with his master's self-image.

Mr Wright elaborated on this theme, explaining that a good dog 'can be ruined by wrong treatment ... A dog is only as good as the person using her ... They are all good-tempered, well-trained dogs, but in a sense their training must continue throughout their working life ... A dog that's ruined cannot easily be retrained, it may have to be sold off. Once it has learned it can take advantage of a blind

23. *Training a guide dog – crossing the road.*

24. *A guide dog in action in a busy street.*

person, it may well do so: a labrador, for instance, if given the chance will often scavenge.'

During their first two days at the Centre the students get used to the layout of the place, they discuss with an instructor their future responsibilities and they carry out exercises designed to familiarise them with the feel of the harness-handle – the instructors taking the part of the dogs. Then comes the long-awaited day when each student is introduced to his future companion – an exciting, nerve-racking, deeply moving occasion. From then on, the students are responsible for the feeding, grooming and exercising of their dogs, and the dogs sleep in their owners' rooms at night. To quote from the Association's leaflet on *Training A Guide Dog*:

'The next few weeks are a testing time for both the instructors and the blind students, especially as the former have to transfer the affection of the dog to its new owner as quickly as possible and encourage an inexperienced and sometimes nervous person to handle a highly trained dog correctly. Instructors combine the roles of canine and human psychologists, preventing any damage being done to the dog's confidence through mis-handling, whilst at the same time correcting the blind student gently and sympathetically.'

The outings are short at first – two half-hours a day – closely supervised; then, as dog and student get to know each other, and the student grows physically fitter, the walks become longer and less closely supervised. 'Towards the end of the course, they can go into town together and cope with traffic, with the instructor only watching from a distance – instead of being ready to grab them, if necessary.'

In essence, the student has to continue all the 'exercises' that the dog has learned. He is in a strange environment, with unfamiliar people – fellow-students, as well as instructors and assistants – in charge of (and in the care of) a valuable, highly-trained, highly responsive companion. The opportunities for errors and mismanagement are manifold. Let me give just two examples of the pitfalls confronting the student.

I watched several students on their first walk with their guide dog accompanied, of course, by their instructor. As the dog sat when she reached the kerb, I noticed that the student – while listening to advice about foot-position, signalling *forward* when the time came, etc., – stood well away from his dog, the harness stretched between the pair. 'Ah yes', said Mr Wright in reply to my query, 'He's afraid of treading on the dog's tail'. Almost all the dogs have long tails, and the blind student has no possible way of telling where the tail may be.

The second example illustrates my own ineptness, as a sighted person in these circumstances. It was explained to me that the owners groom their dogs daily and that they may sometimes have occasion to use a spray on their dog. 'But how do they avoid spraying the dog's eyes?' I asked. 'Oh, these people are acutely aware of eyes', replied my informant, pityingly, 'They cover the dog's eyes with one hand when using the spray'.

By the end of the month the student has learned the rudiments; he has come to trust and rely upon his dog; and, as instructed, to give praise, unstintingly, wherever praise is due. The dog has learned the difference between working with an experienced, sighted instructor and working with her blind owner. She had grown fond of her handler but she had had to share him with half a dozen other dogs. Now she has the undivided attention of her owner and she slowly becomes aware of his need for her. This is not an anthropomorphic statement: the behaviour of guide dogs with their owner in all situations – but especially in a crisis – bears out the truth of the assertion.

When back at home, the owner has to send in to the Training Centre a monthly report on his dog's work and progress. As indicated by Mr Wright, the owner has to continue to reinforce the good behaviour of his dog, throughout her working life. Most dogs, like most people, will become rather lax unless they are constantly encouraged to maintain standards. Several guide dog owners have confirmed that their dog will gradually reduce to mere tokens – or less – the signals which she had been trained to give (and which they need, especially in unfamiliar surroundings), unless she is kept up to the mark with praise and, when necessary, admonition 'Some owners let certain things go and others let others go', a guide dog owner told me, 'but with time there's a certain amount of deterioration in the guiding behaviour of almost all the dogs. You must go on practising them.'

Regular after-care visits are paid by an instructor; and every guide dog has a six monthly check-up from a veterinary surgeon, which includes routine worming. These services are free. The students contribute £1 per week towards accommodation and meals during their month's training at the Centre. Owners who need it receive a financial contribution towards their dog's food. They 'buy' their dog, in the first instance, for the sum of 50 pence. The Association is not subsidised by the state: it is a charity, maintained entirely by voluntary contributions.

When after eight or nine years of work (sometimes longer) the time comes for the dog's retirement, she either stays on as a pet with her owner's family or she may go to a welcoming friend or relative of his. 'The need to replace dogs that retire means that nearly half the places at the Training Centres are taken up by students who have come back for a new dog.' Such students get priority in the queue. They need to be retrained, partly because they must get acquainted with their new dog under supervision, in an environment with which she is familiar; and partly because owner and previous dog, after years together, do really function in all ways as a unit – to an extent which the owner cannot realise until he needs a replacement. To the outside observer, the relationship appears after some years to be positively psychic.

What benefits accrue to the blind, through having a guide dog? They are almost incalculable. The dog becomes her owner's seeing eye; he re-acquires the independence he has lost – or, if he was born blind, had never possessed. He can go virtually anywhere: to work in a factory, into crowded pubs for a drink and a chat, into restaurants or hotels for a meal, to places of worship, up to organ lofts to play or into private houses to tune pianos; he can lead school children on expeditions; he can use any form of public transport.

In addition to the freedom that he now enjoys, he finds that his social life is enormously enhanced. When people see someone with a white stick, they feel *sorry* for them (and pity is not only akin to love, it is akin also to superiority). They either steer clear of the blind with the white stick – 'mustn't get in his way' – or they hasten to help him, say, to cross the road, after which they hasten away. When, however, they see a blind person with his guide dog, they often feel admiration for the efficiency and care shown by the dog, and respect for the confident, self-sufficient, smoothly-moving owner. Such comments as, 'Oh, what a lovely dog – may I pat her?' or 'Gosh, I didn't realise you couldn't see!' are frequent and excellent ice-breakers. The guide dog provides an entrée into society which the blind tend to lack. They are not in a position to make the first advances; the sighted, failing to realise the social isolation of a blind person on his own – and perhaps embarrassed – are often reluctant to make overtures. The guide dog, friendly and equable in temperament, provides an admirable introduction.

If, however, the owner lives alone for choice, is not gregarious and prefers to lead a rather solitary life, he need never feel lonely, for he has with him the ideal, inseparable companion: solicitous, affectionate and loyal – helpfully alert when necessary, but unobtrusive when she is not wanted. The dog herself is happy and fulfilled for she loves her work, she is well cared for, she too enjoys the companionship and she knows that she is needed.

CHAPTER 9

Hearing Dogs for the Deaf

The 'hearing ear' dog sounds at first very similar to the seeing eye dog, but there are important differences between the two. Whilst it is true that in both cases a dog is chosen to afford independence and companionship to an individual lacking in one of the five senses, there the resemblance ends. The guide dog receives a standard course of training and, when ready, his blind owner-to-be is selected to match the trained dog's personality and physique, whereas *the owner* of the hearing dog is selected in advance and his future dog is, as it were, trained to measure – for the needs of the deaf vary from person to person. Also, some persons favour a particular type of dog. One deaf old lady, for instance, expressed a desire for a small white long-coated dog. Others are content to leave the choice of dog to the Training Centre.

Secondly, the hearing dog is usually a stray (and a mongrel) being drawn from one of the animal rescue centres, such as are organised by the National Canine Defence League. Sometimes, however, a private individual will offer a young dog if he can no longer keep it. In that event, the hearing ear dog trainer will go to see the dog in question, to ascertain its suitability for the job. The criteria are as follows: age between eight months and two years, possessing good eyesight, an acute sense of hearing and an appropriate temperament – of which more below.

The dog's size is immaterial, though very big dogs are generally considered unsuitable, for practical reasons. Gender too is immaterial, the bitches being spayed after they have been in season once. The males may or may not be castrated, depending on the circumstances. Although the ratio of dogs to bitches is roughly 50/50 (as is that of the owners) I shall, throughout this chapter, arbitrarily refer to the hearing dog as 'she' and the owner as 'he', simply for the sake of clarity in reading.

Thirdly, the hearing dog, when trained and allocated to her owner, will be on duty 24 hours a day. Unlike the guide dog, she does not wear a special harness – or, indeed, any uniform, to be removed when she is off duty.

Fourthly, whereas guide dogs – like police dogs and sheep dogs – have been used for decades, the concept of hearing dogs for the deaf is relatively new. The project started in 1976, in the U.S.A., and the pilot scheme in Britain (inspired by the American model) was initiated in 1982. Thus the organisers in this country are to some extent still feeling their way. There is no doubt, however, about the viability of the scheme: over 300 dogs have already been successfully placed with hearing-impaired owners in America and these owners are delighted and astonished at the transformation that has been wrought in their daily lives. But owing to the recency of the proposal in Britain, there are still a few problems to be overcome, mainly of an administrative and financial nature. Thus the content of this chapter is less definitive and less categorical than are the contents of the other chapters on working dogs. The organisers are flexible and open-minded about any changes that may have to be made.

Let us first consider the potential owners. They will be either totally deaf or will have severe impairment of hearing. They will be over eighteen years of age and – although they will not necessarily have owned a dog before – they will have a genuine liking for dogs and will be physically and financially capable of looking after their dog. (They will, however, receive some aid with veterinary and feeding costs.) They do not have any other dogs in their house and they live either alone or with another deaf or handicapped person.

These are the guidelines laid down by the Hearing Dogs for the Deaf Training Centre, in conjunction with the Royal National Institute for the Deaf. The relevant facts are ascertained by the Placement Counsellor, Gillian Lacey, an audiologist who interviews potential hearing dog owners, in order to determine their suitability. It is her task to obtain the above information and to evaluate the applicant as a future dog-owner. She has found that many of the potential owners can lip-read, though sometimes they prefer to communicate by writing. Some use sign-language and she, herself, has taken a course in sign-language.

Miss Lacey also assists in the selection and training of the dogs. It is essential that the dogs know and trust the Placement Counsellor, as it is she who acts as liaison officer between dog and owner, when the latter takes over. She also supervises the first week to ten days of dog-plus-owner's life together. For the first three months after placement, regular contact is maintained with recipient and dog; and, if all goes well during this period, a certificate is issued as completion of training.

The master-mind in charge of selection and training is Tony Blunt, who has had 22 years' experience as a dog-trainer in the Police Force. He decides which dogs are likely to prove suitable, by means of specially devised hearing tests and shrewd observation based on very pertinent experience. Since the dog is to serve as her future owner's ears, she must have keen hearing for sounds of varied pitch, timbre and intensity, and she must also be *interested* in sounds and in people. The hearing test, therefore, consists of playing several sounds, one at a time, while the other tester either walks the dog round a field on the lead or has the dog free in a room.

The sounds are, respectively, a squeaker (a soft ball which emits a squeak when pressed: the sort of toy that is popular with babies a few months old – and, indeed, with some puppies); a clicker (noise made by a metal gadget, sounding like a metallic castanet); a bell similar to that of an alarm clock ringing; and a baa or baby type noise (that sounded to me like the sound emitted by an old-fashioned teddy-bear, when pressed in the tummy).

The four sounds are produced in turn, while the dog is being walked or is playing or lying down. Some dogs are scared by one or more of the stimuli and some appear uninterested – briefly pricking an ear, or even ignoring the sound altogether. The correct response for a future dog for the deaf, is sudden and unmistakable: the dog stops walking or playing or dozing as soon as the sound is produced and she rushes towards the source of sound, and eagerly investigates the person from whom the sound appears to emanate. She thus shows herself

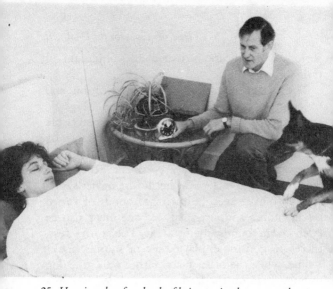

25. *Hearing dog for the deaf being trained to respond to an alarm clock.*

26. *Hearing dog for the deaf being trained to respond to a baby crying.*

to be a good listener and localiser of sound, swift to respond and intrigued by the sound and its source.

The dog's reaction to noises, however, is not the sole criterion: good auditory discrimination and speed of response are necessary but not sufficient. In addition, she needs to have a friendly, extra-verted temperament, to be alert and conscientious and have good powers of concentration, to be energetic, but not over-excitable, placid but not lethargic, neither timid nor nervous. She must like people generally, and be good-humoured and eager to please.

It may be recalled that most of the future hearing dogs are chosen from animal rescue centres. Hence little or nothing is known of their previous experiences, but it is likely that some will have been ill-treated or neglected. If, therefore, some betray signs of fear or suspicion in new surroundings, it is readily understandable – but it still does not augur well for a future hearing dog. On the other hand some of these rescued dogs are so glad to be in touch with a sympathetic human that they easily become attached and, owing perhaps to lingering feelings of insecurity, they are loth to be separated from their new friend. Even when let off the lead in a park, for instance, such dogs will decline to go and explore or to romp with other dogs. They prefer to stay close to their human companion – and this is not a bad trait in a hearing-dog-to-be.

It has been stated that the needs of the deaf vary from person to person. What then are the various functions that the dog may be trained to perform? Let us consider the daily life of a deaf person. He cannot hear the alarm clock that wakes us in the morning (nor can he make use of a flashing light instead, unless he is already awake and looking in the right direction): he cannot hear the front door bell (or buzzer or chimes or knock, as the case may be); nor the whistling of his kettle, nor the cry of the baby, nor the fire alarm, nor the ringing of the telephone. Obviously the dog cannot communicate intelligibly on the telephone, but she can indicate to her owner when the bell is ringing; and people who are hearing-impaired, but not totally deaf, can sometimes understand what is said to them on the telephone if they have a sophisticated electronic device fitted to their telephone which amplifies the speech without distorting it.

There is also the 'TTY system' (Telephone TYping) whereby the deaf who own a TTY machine, can receive and convey telephone messages via a central exchange operator. The latter relays telephonic speech *in typed form* to the deaf person – who in turn, types his reply, which is read over to the caller by the operator (or *typed* back, if the caller is deaf.) Of course not all deaf people are without speech: thus those who have speech and receive the message are able to reply to it orally.

The dog is trained to go to her owner when the telephone bell rings and to inform him, by means of touch, that he is wanted; and she then leads him to the telephone – or to the front door if that is where the ringing comes from, or to the baby if he is crying. These are the two basic tasks that she has to learn: to attract her owner's attention by touch and to lead him to the relevant stimulus – be it crying baby, whistling kettle, buzzer or ringing bell. However, if the fire-alarm sounds, the dog is trained first to contact the owner and then to drop to the ground. The owner then knows that the dog is signalling a fire emergency.

I say attract attention by touch and this vital

phrase requires explanation. The dog will not be heard if she barks; and she will not be seen pricking her ears, unless her owner happens to be watching her. Therefore she has literally to *make contact*, by touching her owner in some way. She may do this by putting her head or paw on his knee, or by nudging him with her muzzle or by jumping up against him or even by circling round him; and once attention has been gained, she leads the way to the source of the noise. During the first weeks of the course, eye contact between dog and trainer is avoided – for if it occurred at an early stage, the dog might well fail to acquire the skill of making bodily contact.

If an unwelcome visitor, such as a burglar, tries to effect an entry, quietly and by some unorthodox means, the dog will be aware of this and will instinctively warn her owner. He, conscious of her sudden alertness, and looking in her direction will note her raised hackles, tensed body and probably her open mouth – for she may well be barking. This presumptive intimation of an intruder is an additional way in ·which the dog's presence promotes her owner's feelings of security and self-confidence. The particular method by which the dog contacts her owner depends on the training she has received. But the trainer will be flexible in this and will be guided by the dog's preferred natural movements. Just as the shepherd will first teach his Collie to drive rightwards if his sheep dog in the first instance approaches the sheep from the left, thus driving the sheep to the right, so the hearing dog trainer will build on the dog's natural use of her paw or her head, and will reinforce that method of contact.

Communication between two animate beings, however, is essentially *two-way*. We must therefore consider the way in which the *owner* is to convey his ideas to the dog. Some deaf people, whilst adept at using sign-language and also, perhaps at lip-reading, are unable to speak audibly. Others, who have been taught to speak, tend to do so in a rather unclear monotone: they have mastered the exceedingly hard task of inferring the consonants and vowels by touching the lips, tongue and throat of their teacher and, having learned these positions, they have learned also to produce some sort of sound. But it is extraordinarily difficult to talk clearly without hearing oneself. We with unimpaired hearing are constantly (unconsciously) getting feedback from hearing what we say and how we say it. This is evident from the way in which people who are going deaf tend to shout as they talk – without realising it.

Thus the dog's owner, even if he has achieved the art of speaking, may be hard to understand – whether by other people or by his dog. For this reason, the trainers of hearing dogs teach them to obey – first the spoken word *plus* arm-signals and, later, to obey arm-signals alone. This applies to the basic training, e.g. *come, sit, stay*. This form of communication has then to be taught to the owner of the dog; and ensuring that owner and dog achieve full mutual understanding is one of the tasks of the Placement Counsellor during the initial period of the dog's life-with-owner.

The training of a dog takes four months and, as stated earlier, she is trained with the needs of one specific deaf person in mind. If her owner-to-be, for instance, is an elderly bachelor, it is unlikely that she will need to learn about the cry of a baby!

If the future owner lives close enough to the Training Centre, he is encouraged to come and watch some of the training. The training sessions consist of four 20-minute sessions per day. These take place in a custom-built private house with sitting-room, bedroom, bathroom and kitchen, since the dog must learn 'home manners' as Mr Blunt puts it, and she must learn too the functions of the various rooms. Most of the rest of the day she spends in kennels, but she goes for walks with Mr Blunt and/or Miss Lacey and she may go and spend an occasional weekend at the house of one or the other. They share the duties of training so that the dog learns to respond to more than one person and will not be put off by the presence of other people.

During the four months training and the early days in her final home, the dog gradually comes to understand her work more fully; and if her owner wishes to inculcate a further skill, she will probably acquire this with relative ease. Someone who already knows four languages will learn a fifth one far more easily and rapidly than will someone with only their native tongue, endeavouring to acquire a second language.

When she goes to live with her owner, the Placement Counsellor will accompany her and will live in the same town or village for the first week to ten days. The Counsellor introduces dog to owner if they have not already met and aims to transfer the affections of the dog from herself to the owner. This cannot be accomplished in a day or two. Dog and owner have to learn to like and trust each other: again, this is a two-way matter. For instance, the owner must learn to sleep with his bedroom door open – or to allow the dog to sleep in his room at night – otherwise she will be unable to fulfil her function as waker-up and, if necessary, as watch-dog at night.

The owner must learn too about the care of his dog: her feeding habits, the importance of grooming and exercising. The Counsellor also introduces the dog plus owner to the vet., and explains about her six-monthly visits to the vet, for check-ups and for inoculation-boosters. By the time the Counsellor leaves town she is satisfied that the two have settled down well and that the dog regards her new abode as her home. The Counsellor makes herself readily available in the future, however, should any problems arise.

The change in the life-style of the owner is very striking. From being psychologically isolated yet dependent, insecure and, alas, to some hearing people figures of fun, the deaf find themselves able to fend for themselves, provided with an ever-ready, alert, affectionate companion who is an object of admiration, which may brush off on to them, and – this too is sometimes good for morale – responsible to a sentient creature who in turn is dependent upon *them*.

There is a great deal of sympathy for the aims of the Hearing Dog movement. This is fortunate for, at this early pilot stage, it costs about £2,500 to train each dog and – like the Guide Dogs – it is a charity and receives no government funds. It is run under the auspices of the R.N.I.D. and is financed through the good offices of various sponsors, such as Pedigree Petfoods, Pebble Mill at 1.0, PRO-Dogs and Mutual (Insurance) of New York. The Girl Guides, Cubs and Scouts of Greater London have also contributed. The British Small Animal Veterinary Association provides free vaccination and annual boosters, and Pet Plan offers insurance against illness and accidents to cover the first year. Despite these instances of generosity, the work at present is operating virtually on a shoe string, and it could proceed far faster and on a bigger scale if more funds were available.

CHAPTER 10

The Dog as Therapist

A therapist is someone who treats an individual or a group needing care, in an endeavour to make them feel better. If one *feels* better, one usually *is* better, in the sense that physical improvement is likely to follow psychological improvement. And if the illness is itself psychological, such as depression, or feelings of inferiority, isolation or helplessness, then feeling better is indeed the beginning of a cure.

It follows that the therapist in the chapter-heading is one who treats the persons needing help, in an attempt to ameliorate their condition, whatever it may be. Are we justified then in designating the dog as therapist? If we are interested in the *results* of treatment, it has to be conceded that the dog is, in many cases, a successful therapist. Indeed other pets too have this quality of helping human beings: not only dogs but cats, horses, budgerigars and hamsters sometimes play their part.

It should be noted, however, that the dog as therapist is not analogous to the police dog or the sheep dog. These are selected and trained for particular purposes, whereas the dog therapist acts as such by virtue of his own nature. He is not trained for the task: indeed, it would be difficult to envisage such training since his therapeutic qualities reside in his flexibility, his responsiveness and his sensitivity to the moods and needs of his human companion(s). He does not therefore have specific tasks to learn. A great deal of his therapeutic value resides in his just being there and making few or no demands.

Guide dogs for the blind and hearing dogs for the deaf also act as therapists to some extent. We have seen how they instil confidence and provide companionship for people who need these even more than the rest of us. But the guide dogs and hearing dogs' major tasks are to play the part of seeing eyes and listening ears. This chapter deals with the dog simply as therapist: i.e. with the fact that the dog aids people who are physically or mentally ill, or pathologically lonely or incapable of adjusting to fellow human beings.

First, the evidence: 'Pet ownership proved the strongest social predictor of survival for one year after hospital treatment'. The research yielding this information was conducted on patients who had been hospitalised for severe heart disease. Doctors Katcher and Friedmann were concerned primarily with the role of human relationships but they included in their study one question on pet ownership – with the above surprising results.

If, however, the facts are examined in detail, those results lose something of their surprise-value. Most people who keep a dog, *like* dogs or, if this is an over-statement, at least they like their own dog. Since they like their dog, they tend to talk to it, caress it and play with it. Evidently stroking a dog is good for the stroker as well as being enjoyable for the dog. Patients with raised blood pressure and with heart conditions fare better if they own a dog of which they are fond. 'It has been known for some time that stroking a pet dog reduces that dog's blood pressure', but it has now been established that greeting and petting your dog 'causes your blood pressure to drop below *the resting level*' [my italics]. More generally, 'Being in the presence of a pet has beneficial effects on (the owner's) heart function.'

We all need play of some kind, whatever our age. Play enables us to concentrate on something other than ourselves; it both stimulates and relaxes us, and some people have difficulty in relaxing either on their own or with other people. But those with a pet dog will play with it – throwing a ball, patting it, tickling it, talking to it without expectation of audible reply – and will thus relax, albeit unwittingly. They will behave like this only if they are fond of dogs but then we do not fare all that well medically if we do not like our (human) physician. Those who leave the surgery muttering: 'He never listens to a word I say', or 'Wish she'd *tell* me what is wrong', or 'That's the third time he's asked me how old I am – it should be in his notes', or 'She really should try to cultivate some sort of bedside manner' – such patients do not thrive as well as those who like and who have confidence in their doctor. So our regard for our dog is part of his competence as a therapist.

His very presence incites us to play, to fondle, to talk to him and to laugh with him – and the therapeutic effects of laughter are well known.

How does a dog elicit this behaviour? What is his secret strategy that causes us to treat him in this unique way? – for there are few, if any, human companions with whom we unwind like this, expecting *and getting* instant understanding and sympathy, and never being let down. His secret lies in his ineffable trust in his owner. He believes his owner to be the most wonderful thing that ever happened, and makes this clear to everyone: he happens to possess a godlike owner. This is very good for morale.

The owner is accepted unconditionally: whatever he does or says is right. If the dog had had a divergent view on some topic, he readjusts. If he is accidentally stepped on, *he* apologises for being in the way. He is unquenchably forgiving, uncritically receptive, loyal, welcoming and more perceptive than are many humans, despite the faculty of language shared by them and owner. He has an uncanny way of understanding when owner is depressed or anxious. He makes it clear that he recognises the existence of some trouble: he offers to share it, while at the same time intimating that matters might be worse.

I said earlier that we talk to dogs without expectation of audible reply. This should now be amplified. In the first place it is restful: we know that a dog will listen to us but we know, too, that he will not answer back. Which of us does not enjoy having the last word? He does, however, reply in his own inaudible fashion. He brings into play the armoury of normal behaviours described in Chapters 2 and 3. By means of his ears, his tail, his eyes, his whole body, he conveys, 'I understand' – and this again is therapeutic for owner.

The dog's understanding of what goes on is not confined to what his owner tells him. If his owner picks up keys or handbag, opens a desk or kitchen door, scratches his head, changes his shoes, sighs, lights a cigarette, switches on the television, looks at his watch ... all such actions are observed by the dog – though owner himself may be unaware of them or their import. He interprets these actions and is always willing to co-operate, unless he is ill or very old. Indeed, even a dog who is unwell will make the effort to help, if he feels needed.

There are two further ways in which the dog functions as therapist. He provides an acceptable, and often necessary, outlet for human emotions. Whether his owner is feeling affectionate or humorous, elated or in a rage, his canine companion is at hand, ready to act as a safety valve. It is not very pleasant for the dog when his owner, having lost his temper swears at him or throws a shoe at him. But the dog comes to know that this crisis will pass, that his owner is merely letting off steam and – like the rest of us – the dog would rather be cursed than ignored. And he can take any amount of loving overtures: he is most unlikely to indicate that enough is enough or that he is not in the mood when owner caresses him in an access of loneliness or of frustrated affection or even in a sudden burst of tears.

The physical contact between owner and pet is comforting. Many people experience the need to touch and be touched by another sentient being, but all too many lack the opportunity. Some live alone and have few or no intimate friends or relatives. Others are so much aware of the importance of touch that they are self-conscious about it: they dare not initiate even the most casual physical contact, for fear of rebuff and – since they fail to initiate it – they give the impression of fastidiously preferring to remain invoilate. The dog is very valuable for such people: he will clearly request close contact and revel in it, with – as we have seen – beneficial results for himself and owner.

Similarly with speech: people who are mentally ill or handicapped sometimes have difficulty in talking to other people. In some cases, they may have remained silent for months or years. This is not wilful obstinacy. They *cannot* bring themselves to speak and they may suffer intolerably in their silence. The introduction of a pet may work apparent miracles in such cases. The patient finds himself talking to the animal, who in turn responds – favourably – and a vicious circle may be broken. When talking to a pet you cannot get it wrong: whatever is said, the animal will evince interest and pleasure – thus reinforcing the habit of speech in the patient.

In our culture, talking aloud to oneself is regarded as odd, a first sign of madness, but talking to animals is socially acceptable. The presence of a pet helps also to break the ice between strangers, or a couple of extreme introverts or people who are psychiatrically ill. The mentally disturbed are often very diffident; their confidence has been eroded and they lack the modicum of self-esteem inherent in most other people. But such patients will display a touching pride in the poise of their pet cat or the intelligence of their dog. This sometimes marks the beginning of a healthier attitude to themselves.

Also salutory is the fact that their pet needs them; it depends on them for food and exercise and grooming. The dog reawakens in the patient his dormant sense of responsibility and of nurturance. The patient responds to this need and, as a result, may manage to go for walks again, first forcing himself and later, perhaps, enjoying the fresh air and exercise. Purpose and order re-enter his life, with *him* in charge, and this has a reassuring effect.

The therapeutic effects of pets has been officially recognised by hard-headed authority during recent years and they are now welcomed in certain mental hospitals and institutions for the disturbed and the handicapped. The benefits of horse-riding for physically and mentally disabled children are now widely accepted. Autistic children – who are pathologically withdrawn and have great difficulty in communicating with people – respond particularly well to the presence of a pet. Dogs seem to recognise young children as such and to accept their occasionally disconcerting behaviour and, in the same way, they make allowances for the mentally ill. But apart from his increased tolerance with the young or disturbed, the dog continues to take them seriously; he does not patronise them one moment and ignore them the next – as some people are prone to do. And the disturbed who are, at some level, sensitive and observant, appreciate this treatment from their pets.

It would be absurd to suggest that the presence of a pet dog (or cat or rabbit) is a panacea for all ills, mental and physical, or for all unwilling solitaries. A hospital overrun with lively animals would become a shambles; and, if they were kept in cages they would be miserable – and lose their value as therapists. A person (call him John), living alone in unhappy solitude, complaining of lack of companionship and an over-sedentary life-style, may well find that a dog helps to fill the void and to afford him exercise. But if John does not care for dogs or cannot summon the energy to take one for walks, the venture will not be a success for either participant.

Cats are less demanding than dogs, they do not require exercising, they groom themselves, have impeccable excretory habits given adequate facilities and they can fulfil many of the functions of the pet-therapist. Stroking them gives aesthetic as well as sensual pleasure, they are graceful in movement and in repose, and they *purr* – an endless source of satisfaction to cat-lovers. John might do better to have a cat – providing he is prepared to take responsibility for feeding it – and this entails shopping – and either supplying its toilet-tray with daily-changed cat-litter or giving it the opportunity to leave and re-enter the house at will.

The institutions that appreciate the therapeutic value of dogs and other animals for some of their inmates, have found that the advantages greatly outweigh the drawbacks. These include hospitals and mental hospitals, nursing homes, old people's homes, children's homes – and prisons. In prisons the animals are liable to be fish and budgerigars or small animals such as guinea-pigs and hamsters. When these were introduced into the hospital wing of a prison it was found that 'the level of violence – always high – dropped significantly, prisoners made fewer suicide attempts and their medication require-ments decreased ... So far there have been no instances of animal abuse in the prison ... It is felt that no-one would dare to harm a pet for fear of retribution from the other prisoners.'

We have now briefly reviewed the case of the dog as therapist. Unlike the other 'helping' dogs in this book – who aid the blind and the deaf, the police and the shepherd – the dog as therapist receives no training. He plays a therapeutic role unwittingly, by virtue of his nature. His behaviour is intuitive, though with experience he does learn to modify it. Not all dogs turn out to be good therapists but the proportion of successful dog-therapists in the canine population is high.

As we have seen, pets other than dogs also have a therapeutic role to play, but that of the dog is probably the most active. It is not suggested that pets should *replace* psychiatrists and nurses but that they can provide valuable additional aid in public institutions and in private houses, for the sick, the borderline sick and the officially normal. One of the virtues of animals is that they do not discriminate between these groups in their feelings or their behaviour.

CHAPTER 11

The Dog as Nuisance

I have sung the praises of the dog as worker in this book. Probably most of my readers will be what have been described as 'dog people', that is, they will like dogs in general, be aware of their virtues and be eager to increase their understanding of the dog.

Not all people, however, fall into the category of 'dog people'. Some have a strong antipathy towards dogs and say, 'No, I hate dogs – nasty, smelly creatures, always yapping, leaving hairs all over the place, fouling the street, worrying farm-animals, spreading disease, biting people, causing traffic accidents and propagating rabies. They really ought to be banned.'

How much truth is there in these allegations? As with most generalisations of a derogatory nature these are to some extent factually based – although a great many of the anti-dog brigade have an innate antipathy to dogs, which they rationalise by invoking these criticisms. Few will admit that they simply dislike – or fear – dogs, even quiet, clean, well-mannered ones, and so they adopt the familiar method of voicing objections which sound reasonable and can be substantiated up to a point.

'There are no problem children' it is often said, 'only problem parents'. This applies even more strongly to dogs: there are many problem owners in the sense that they do not train or discipline their dogs, and this results in unpleasant, and sometimes dangerous, behaviour, as for instance, when dogs cause traffic accidents. Such dogs get themselves a bad name; indeed, they *deserve* a bad name – but through no fault of their own.

Let us consider the various objections that have been raised. 'Dogs are smelly'. A characteristic doggy smell does emanate from the majority of dogs – large or small, smooth-haired or rough-haired – if they are in poor health or are not groomed regularly. Some dog-owners do not mind the smell (and some do not notice it) but the more fastidious find it distasteful. Almost certainly, if the dog is an indoor dog, some of their friends will object to the smell; and, if they themselves do not own a dog, they may think it is inevitable.

Dogs should be groomed regularly in any case, for their own good, the requisite frequency varying with the breed and the individual. Old dogs tend to suffer from bad breath, and to generate unpleasant smells to a greater extent than the young and the middle-aged. (These disabilities are not confined to canines). If a dog is regularly dusted against the lie of his coat, and rubbed with one of the proprietory cleansing and anti-parasite powders designed for domestic animals (*not* with DDT) and then combed and brushed, he will lose his doggy smell – and any others that humans find undesirable. Interestingly enough, this does not render him unacceptable to other dogs – unless a positively scented powder is used: this I do not recommend.

Regular grooming will also minimise the problem of 'leaving hairs all over the place'. All dogs moult – with the exception of the curly-coats, such as poodles and curly retrievers. The official moulting seasons are Spring and Autumn, at which times the dog's coat is said to be preparing, respectively, for warm, sunny weather (requiring a lighter-weight coat) and for cold, wetter weather (requiring a heavier coat). But, as more than one owner has ruefully complained to me: 'The books know that and *I* know that – but our dog doesn't seem to know it! He moults practically all the year round.'

Frequent brushing and combing helps with this problem. If the owner greatly dislikes the presence of hairs on carpets and clothing, he might consider getting a curly-coated dog next time. And if certain friends strongly object, he really should leave the dog at home when he goes to visit these particular friends. If he dislikes finding hairs on the furniture, it is of course up to him to train the dog from puppyhood to keep off chairs, sofas, etc.

'Always yapping' is the way anti-dog people stereotype small dogs. It suggests high-pitched vocalisation occurring very frequently – and especially when visitors (or tradesmen or postmen) come to the house. It is true that many miniature and 'toy' dogs, such as Yorkshire Terriers, Chihuahuas and Dachshunds, do this and also some slightly larger dogs, such as Corgies. Medium-sized and big dogs do not yap but they too may give tongue vociferously when anyone enters the house – or even approaches it.

This is a difficult habit to break, and many dog-owners maintain, quite convincingly, that one of their reasons for keeping a dog is as a deterrent to thieves. 'But surely you don't think *that's* going to keep burglars away' exclaims a member of the anti-dog brigade, pointing to the Chihuahua and wincing ostentatiously at each burst of yapping. He is mistaken, however. It is not just Alsatian and

Dobermann households that deter burglars: they fear the *noise* created by a dog – at whatever pitch. It is often stated that keeping a dog is the most effective method of burglar-prevention. They may not be afraid of the Jack Russell or the Pekinese, but they do fear the alarm raised by any dog. Burglars tend to prefer dogless houses and flats.

It is of course one thing to have a dog that barks at the illegal entry of a stranger and another to have a dog that barks indiscriminately at any and every stimulus. Neighbours, as well as guests, are apt to complain about the latter habit; it is trying even for the owners, after a time.

If your dog does delight to bark, say *no!* when he does so at inopportune moments, and, if he persists, put him in a room by himself for a few minutes. Do not let him out *when he is barking.* He will dislike being deprived of your company and, in due course, he should understand what you want. On the other hand, if he is a non-barker and he usually fails to give tongue even when people enter the house – then reward him with praise and a pat and perhaps a dog-biscuit on the rare occasions when he does emit a bark at the right time, until he gets the idea; then gradually tail off the rewards.

There is one species of dog, officially – and correctly – known as barkless. This is the Basenji, a hunting dog from Central Africa, with a rather charming, Disney-esque appearance. He is said to utter a 'soft cry which is a mixture of a chortle and a yodel'. In addition to being barkless, Basenjis are exceptionally hard to train and are liable to wander. They are not, therefore, ideal pets for this country, nor are they ideal watch-dogs.

We now come to the more serious objections to dogs – their fouling of pavements and recreation grounds and, allied to this unpleasantness, their spreading of disease among young children, through their faeces. (Insofar as they do spread disease in this way, through certain worms which are sometimes contained in their excreta, children are not necessarily the only sufferers. But the anti-dog brigade, knowing the certain results that follow any mention of dangers *to children* are liable to stress these particular risks and enthusiastically to overstate them).

Such risks do however, exist. Young children are closer to the ground than adults and they are more likely to suck their fingers. They may do themselves harm in this way – or even by putting their fingers in their mouths after having stroked a puppy who has worm-eggs on his coat. (They may, of course, ingest other noxious substances if they habitually suck their fingers, but anti-dog people tend to ignore this fact).

The solution to this menace is twofold, and, once again, it depends on the dog-owners. They should ensure that their dog or puppy is free from worms, by consulting their vet. He should be able to advise them whether their dog does have worms and, if so, what kind they are and how to rid him of them. There are many types – some of which are entirely harmless to human beings. Owners can also help themselves, by inspecting their dog's faeces from time to time – though this is not a completely foolproof method of discovering whether the dog is worm-infested. The best plan is to worm your dog every six months, or as recommended by your vet. The worming tablets are safe and inexpensive, and obtainable from vet, or pet-shop – but pet shops are naturally less expert at diagnosis and treatment than are vets.

It is worthwhile keeping your dog free from worms for everyone's sake. The dog himself, is better off without worms: he will look better, feel better and eat better if he is free from them. The appetite of a dog with worms tends to be capricious.

The second solution is of course to ensure that your dog does not do his business in places used by the public – especially recreation grounds and city pavements. Many dogs, as they emerge from puppyhood, develop a sense of propriety in this respect. They manage to control themselves until they see a piece of waste-ground or rubble, a closely packed group of bushes, a tip or unfrequented bit of their owner's garden – which they then proceed to use a lavatory. But not all dogs possess this awareness; not all owners have gardens; and not all towns have suitable areas readily available. Most dogs who do not take to this behaviour naturally, can be trained to do so.

The official ruling is that in town dogs must use the gutter for this purpose but, unfortunately, it is not unknown for dogs to be run over when performing. Some drivers are callous and others simply do not see the dog if it is small or visibility is poor. I, myself, know of three dogs that have been run over in this way. I therefore do not advocate training the dog to use the gutter – nor do I advocate the fouling of pavements. Until the dog has learnt what areas are permissible, I think his walker should arm himself with a suitable implement – a flat stone, say, or a piece of cardboard, or one of the scoops sold for this purpose – and transfer the excrement from pavement to gutter. The refuse thus littering the gutter will compare quite favourably with the broken glass, banana-and orange-peel, sweet-papers, cigarette cartons and flattened coke cans that at present deface our streets – all, needless to say, deposited by the 'higher animals'. Moreover excreta, unlike these, is biodegradable.

The worrying of farm-animals is a very serious matter and accounts for the intolerance of many country people towards unfamiliar dogs. Thousands of sheep are ruined every year by dogs whose urban owners let them range the countryside, off the lead and uncontrolled. Some maul the sheep so badly that they have to be destroyed; some dogs will actually savage a sheep to death; some race after them at such a pace that the sheep are terrified and made ill; and sometimes a chasing dog will cause a sheep to fall and land on its back – from which position it cannot rise and will die, if not promptly rescued. Pregnant ewes, when harried, are liable to drop their lambs. Chickens also suffer from the attentions of uncontrolled dogs.

The situation has become so bad that the law has recently been changed. In the past, a farmer had the legal right to shoot a dog on his land, if he observed it molesting his animals. But now he is entitled to shoot any dog that he sees on his land, whether or not it is doing any obvious harm. An inevitable result is that sometimes a perfectly innocent dog will get shot – its owner naturally being furiously indignant. But the fault does lie with the owners. They should realise that their dogs must either be held on the lead, or if free, must be kept within sight throughout a country walk, and strictly under their control.

The same considerations apply to dogs who cause traffic accidents. In many towns it is decreed that dogs must be kept on the lead when being walked. This has the dual aim of preventing accidents and pavement-fouling. But many owners ignore this ruling – ignoring too the fact that their dog may at any moment dive off the pavement, oblivious of traffic – perhaps to investigate an interesting scent, perhaps to pick up a tempting bit of food, perhaps to pursue a bitch on heat. Not only is the dog liable to get hurt, but pedestrians and drivers are put at risk. If dog-owners insist on letting their dogs run free, they must train them to instant obedience and inculcate a strong traffic-sense.

The irresistible attraction of an appropriate female for most male dogs is notorious. The urge is so intense that dogs have been known to walk many miles, to jump out of first-floor windows, even to jump *through* a plate-glass window, in hot pursuit. This again, is a fact to which dog-owners should be alerted.

In particular the owners of non-spayed bitches should behave responsibly in the matter. It is culpable to let one's bitch walk out of the house and, in due course, walk back home – when she is in season. Not only will she attract a host of followers on the walk, but the house is likely to be besieged by suitors for days on end. If she is of liftable size, it helps to carry her for the first fifty yards or so, on leaving the house and again for the last fifty yards on returning. The vet. will supply scent-eliminating or scent-reducing medication, though this is not always wholly effective. He can, however, give medications which will postpone, or even prevent, the bitch's coming on heat. The feasibility of having your dog spayed after one season – if you do not intend to breed from her – should be considered.

The accusation that dogs bite is serious but not well-founded. Very few dogs who have been sensibly treated do bite or snap. Some will do so if severely provoked, though such behaviour is rare. Legally, every dog is entitled to one bite (of a human being) and if this occurs again he must be put down. But a dog who bites once without provocation is likely to do so again. If your dog does bite or snap, you should urgently consider having him destroyed before he does any further damage. It is a heart-rending decision, for you may well be devoted to each other – and your dog would probably never dream of attacking his owner. He can, however, be put down swiftly and painlessly by the vet. and this will save you – and perhaps other people – endless anxiety. A dog whose temper cannot be relied upon is a menace and one such animal provides effective ammunition for the anti-dog brigade.

Finally, the suggestion that dogs propagate rabies: this has no factual basis at present in Britain – thanks to our stringent quarantine regulations. Every animal legally imported into this country has to spend six months in quarantine, where it is well treated, well fed and housed, but it entails of course a long separataion – although visits to the dog are permitted. Initially he feels lonely and bereaved. Some owners of small pets are foolhardy enough to smuggle their animals into the country in order to avoid the long period of quarantine.

This conduct cannot be too strongly deprecated. The smugglers are not only foolhardy and selfish, they are literally criminal. It is thanks to these strict rules that rabies has been unknown in Britain for decades, and one imported case of the dread disease could cause anguish to thousands of families – and their dogs who would, at best, have to be muzzled. Would that it were as easy to train owners as it is to train dogs!

CHAPTER 12

Understanding Involves Training

If a dog's behaviour is annoying or dangerous, this is usually the fault of the owner. The evident unwillingness of many dog-owners to train their pets, once house-training has been effected, is strange in view of the fact that, if a little trouble is taken, most dogs can be trained in essentials in a few months. Those owners who allow their dogs to roam the streets, to bark incessantly, to chase cats and farm animals – in a word, to act uncontrollably both at home and abroad – must be lazy or foolish or unimaginative. Such owners have the temerity to assert that 'My dog is too intelligent to be obedient – he is so full of his own ideas and interests, he has no time for ours'!

Insofar as there is a relationship between a dog's intelligence and his trainability, it goes the other way: the more intelligent dog tends to learn more concepts and skills and to learn them faster, than the duller dog. But there are very few dogs who are incapable of acquiring the basic habits that are necessary if he, his owner and their neighbours are to lead a peaceful, nuisance-free life.

Come (in response to the word or to a whistle), *sit, lie down, stay, heel, drop it, wait, down* and *no!* are the main essentials. If your dog also learns to obey *fetch, carry, say please* and *shut the door*, these may prove useful but it does not *matter* if he fails to master them. If he does not learn the earlier commands, however, he will not be under your control and, sooner or later, trouble may ensue. The trouble may take the form of your dog getting lost, or knocking someone downstairs or barking non-stop, or unseating a motor-cyclist, or swallowing some object not designed for ingestion; or it may take the form of having to keep your dog perpetually on the lead in the park, or periodically having to shut him in house or car, on his own. In either case, he will feel thwarted and his owners may feel failures.

If your dog should get lost or run away for a time, don't beat him or scold him when he gets back – for he will then be less willing to return next time. Make him extra welcome when he brings himself home, but try to prevent a recurrence of the incident: it may become a habit and you have, of course, no jurisdiction over him when he is out of your sight.

It is worth taking some care over your dog's training for your own sake as well as everybody else's. The watchwords are patience, kindness and consistency. He must first learn his name – which most dogs pick up very quickly. Then proceed with the other words, rewarding him with praise and a pat when he responds correctly. Give him plenty of practice but do not go on too long with any one lesson. Use short simple words of command to begin with and, later, if you wish, you can address him in phrases or whole sentences. He will learn to understand *both* the tone of voice *and* the actual words. Dogs who are talked to a great deal become impressively adept at following a conversation – and even at eavesdropping when people are talking to one another. Such dogs are apt to appear quite perturbed, if people in their presence begin speaking in a different language.

For owners who do not take easily to dog-training, or who have acquired an untrained dog long past puppyhood, it may be a good idea to take him to local dog-training classes. Almost all towns nowadays run such courses. Most of the establishments offer several levels of training.

These centres have a number of advantages. The trainers take about ten or twelve dog-plus-owners in each class. They are usually people who have had a lot of experience with dogs of all breeds and who therefore have good understanding of each dog as an individual and of his relationship with his owner. Furthermore, the dog will become used to meeting other dogs, at close quarters, at the classes. None of them will be feeling territorially minded as none of them is on his home ground. The dog who is suspicious or snappy or scared of other dogs will soon perceive that all are friendly and all are equal at this place, and this in itself is educative for difficult dogs. It is also instructive for the owner to see the methods used and it is morale-boosting to observe that there are other dogs as lacking in discipline as his own.

It should be stressed, however, that the weekly or bi-weekly sessions do not *replace* the daily instruction that your dog should receive at home. The sessions may hasten the process and they may enlighten the owner as to the most suitable methods to employ. But it is vital to do homework with your dog, otherwise the time and money spent on the classes will be largely wasted. Indeed, without homework, the dog may gain the impression that sitting on command, or walking to heel, or whatever, are processes that go on at the centre and only at the centre. It would be like giving a child a weekly piano lesson and never getting her to practise between lessons.

With or without professional training courses, your dog should gradually become socialised and controllable, and build up his recognition vocabulary, so that by the time he is six-twelve months, he knows what is going on, he knows what is expected of him and he co-operates willingly. In training your dog, you are learning to understand him – and he is learning to understand you. While you are educating him, he is educating you, although neither of you may be aware of this at the time. You cannot understand your dog's behaviour unless you see it in the context of his training and this is to some extent a reciprocal matter.

In addition to training, your dog needs regular exercising, feeding and grooming. It is good for him, too, to have the opportunity of making social contact with other dogs – and with people other than his owner. If he has a varied and interesting life – meeting people and visiting new places – he is, himself, likely to become more interesting. Dogs are immensely accommodating, however, and if their owner leads a solitary, monotonous life – whether unavoidably or for preference – they will adapt to this way of life, providing they receive the exercise and the occasional small talk that keeps them responsive.

Most dogs actively enjoy carrying out the commands they have learnt, if they have been trained with kindness. It will be remembered that the professional trainers and handlers all stressed the importance of teaching by means of praise where this is due. Few, if any, use chastisement; and none use punishment so severe that the dog becomes fearful: this may prove self-defeating and, in any case, it means that your dog will not take the pleasure in obeying commands that a humanely trained dog will do. Fear and pain are poor teachers.

I have friends who laugh derisively at me during the period that I am training a new puppy – 'so strict ... so rigid ... so time-consuming' they murmur pityingly. A year or so later the same friends will express their envy that I happen to possess such an intelligent and well-mannered dog who stays at home uncomplainingly when so requested and remains in the back of the car when taken for a drive not leaping into the road as the car door is opened. The admired intelligence and obedience are mainly the result of careful training while the dog is young and impressionable.

If you own a pet dog, or wish to own one, it is essential to understand his behaviour, and for him to understand yours. This mutual understanding derives largely from his upbringing. The odds are that an ill-trained puppy will become a nuisance dog. Don't let this happen – do train him to become an intelligent and well-mannered dog.